W9-CBH-268

Flann O'Brien's
Exorbitant Novels

Flann O'Brien's Exorbitant Novels

Thomas F. Shea

Lewisburg
Bucknell University Press
London and Toronto: Associated University Presses

Associated University Presses
440 Forsgate Drive
Cranbury, NJ 08512

Associated University Presses
25 Sicilian Avenue
London WC1A 2QH, England

Associated University Presses
P.O. Box 39, Clarkson Pstl. Stn.
Mississauga, Ontario,
L5J 3X9 Canada

The paper used in this publication meets the requirements
of the American National Standard for Permanence of Paper
for Printed Library Materials Z39.48-1984.

Library of Congress Cataloging-in-Publication Data

Shea, Thomas F., 1953–
   Flann O'Brien's exorbitant novels / Thomas F. Shea.
     p.   cm.
   Includes bibliographical references and index.
   ISBN 0-8387-5220-9 (alk. paper)
   1. O'Brien, Flann, 1911–1966—Criticism and interpretation.
I. Title.
PR6029.N56Z87   1992
823'.914—dc20   91-58168
                                           CIP

PRINTED IN THE UNITED STATES OF AMERICA

To Pegi

Contents

Acknowledgments

Evelyn O'Nolan has made this book possible, not only through her continuing support, but by graciously allowing me to quote freely from her late husband's letters, manuscripts, and published works. The staff of the National Library, Dublin; Special Collections, Morris Library, Southern Illinois University; and The Harry Ransom Humanities Research Center, University of Texas, have assisted me and made my research enjoyable. Permission to quote previously published material has been granted by Walker and Company, *Notes on Modern Irish Literature*, and *Colby Library Quarterly.*

I want to thank Richard Poirier, Julian Moynahan, and John Richetti, who helped me to shape my first explorations of O'Brien. All of my colleagues at the University of Connecticut have been most supportive, especially Clare Virginia Eby, Arnold Orza, and William Rosen. Special thanks go out to Michael Meyer, Lee Jacobus, and William Sheidley, who read the manuscript during its later stages and advised me well. Throughout the years, numerous daring students have inspired me and prompted fruitful risk taking. Several grants from the Research Foundation, University of Connecticut, have enabled me to complete the research for this book. The editorial department at Associated University Presses has been wonderfully helpful throughout the bookmaking process.

I remain continually obliged to William F. Shea and Alice L. Shea for minding what they were about when they begot me. I am especially grateful to and appreciative of my wife, Pegi, whose energy and humor have made working with Flann O'Brien even more fun.

Introduction

Since the debut of *At Swim-Two-Birds* in 1939, Flann O'Brien's novels have delighted and perplexed generations of readers with tastes for creative havoc. But while praise has been plentiful, serious scholarly criticism has been lacking. I intend to remedy this deficiency by analyzing O'Brien's novelistic career in the light of previously neglected material: his early prose experiments written for *Comhthrom Feinne* and *Blather*, two unpublished manuscripts of *At Swim-Two-Birds*, and his unpublished letters which reveal some of the hidden authorial strategies of the man behind the masks.

O'Brien's texts significantly "re-imagine" the novel and confront, under the guise of mere fun, many of the major literary "issues" generated by the linguistic and fictional theories of the last half century. It would be reductive, however, merely to accommodate O'Brien's novels to convenient tags such as Shklovsky's "defamiliarization," Bakhtin's "carnivalization," Derrida's *"différance,"* Barthes's "myth," or Kristeva's "semiotic activity." The unique voices and narrative strategies emerging through O'Brien's novels are best appreciated on their own terms.

The texts written during the 1930s, especially *At Swim-Two-Birds* and *The Third Policeman*, anticipate many current critical concerns, especially theories of the novel, while the fictions of the 1960s, *The Hard Life* and *The Dalkey Archive*, strenuously resist many of the literary perspectives O'Brien considered "exegetic nonsense." *An Béal Bocht* (1941), "edited by Myles na Gopaleen," should be left for the Irish scholar daring enough to tackle its complex parodies of Gaelic stylists such as Tomás Ó Criomhthainn and Séamas Ó Grianna. It is essential to remember that, while he lived, O'Brien refused to allow his Gaelic *divarsions* to be misconstrued in any English translation.

Eight years prior to the publication of *At Swim-Two-Birds*, Flann O'Brien launched his writing career with a satiric essay in University College, Dublin's student magazine. Between 1931 and 1935, first in the university publication *Comhthrom Feinne* and then in his own magazine *Blather*, O'Brien emerges as a subversive, experimental craftsman with words. Although neglected or dismissed by most critics, these early inquisitive inventions deserve serious scrutiny; they often display several significant impulses which inform O'Brien's subsequent novels. Many of these compositions manifest his penchant for parodying literary and nonliterary conventions as well as his flair for trying out types of talk to test their resiliencies through creative distortions. From the beginning, O'Brien's self-conscious sense of style as performance prompts him to mask his identity behind a myriad of pseudonyms. Behind protective posings—most notably Brother Barnabus and Count O'Blather—the young man whose mother baptized him Brian O'Nolan experiments with the precarious instabilities of creating a self through unstable styles. These early compositions also reveal O'Brien's emerging skepticism of an author's power to beget. He seems to seek out verbal obstacles and narrative occasions to test the degree to which tangible textual dictates, such as the materiality of language or covert rules of discourse, may usurp a writer's authority.

At Swim-Two-Birds (1939), O'Brien's first and most exorbitant novel, comically exempts itself from traditional systems of narrative coherence. Structurally, it repeatedly wrestles with time, disrupting our usual senses of priority, causality, and development. The text resists conventional strategies for finding (or making) "meaning" as O'Brien involves the reader in self-conscious, self-enabling, self-threatening negotiations with language. *At Swim* further exhibits O'Brien's uneasiness with the idea of an author as the origin or source of a statement, his disillusionment with the naive assurance that naming corresponds with control. The early, unpublished manuscripts of *At Swim*, composed between 1934 and 1938, are essential for a full appreciation of the novel; they reveal O'Brien in the act of constructing, reimagining, and radically revamping his first novel. Through these early manuscripts, we witness him experimenting with the activity of inscribing and testing the volatile, unreliable propensities of words, styles, and narrative arrangements.

In *At Swim*, O'Brien also explores word games and Irish traditions of verbal magic to stress the precariousness of writing. The Finn MacCool and Mad Sweeny sections, especially, emphasize traditions of recitation rather than reading. They dramatize how certain sounds may call forth neighboring sounds, determining the direction and content of discourse. Medieval oral traditions are also smuggled into inappropriate modern contexts, distorting a variety of contemporary styles. Through verbal refraction and displacement, O'Brien competes with the contorting inclinations inherent in all modes of expression.

The Third Policeman, written a year after *At Swim*, examines the potential of transgression for affirming and perhaps "re-inscribing" a self. The novel focuses on an unnamed, nonexistent narrator who finds himself in a bizarre environment where none of the "normal" cognitive operations hold true. In this twilight zone, the procedures of language through which he has learned to make sense of "himself" and "the world" are abruptly invalidated. The narrator's agitated confusions prompt him to question how his existence—and ultimately the reader's existence—is caught up in the ability to name and be named. In response to his predicament, he probes irregular sorts of coherence, different methods of amalgamation, and modified criteria of communication. Through permutations of phrase making, newerfangled arrangements of words, and transgressive metaphors, he discovers the animating charge of initiating innovation. And, most significantly, when language confirms his death, he counterpunches by talking and writing. Silence should be the most appropriate expression for a man with no name who does not exist. Yet we are paradoxically treated to the complicated, invigorating verbal transgressions of a voice articulating a self as it tells us it is not there.

O'Brien's last two novels, *The Hard Life* (1961) and *The Dalkey Archive* (1964), share several attributes. Both were written twenty-odd years after the earlier novels; both appear unusually tame for O'Brien; and both are often taken lightly as enervated, end-of-career efforts by an author who once had good stuff. However, O'Brien's unpublished letters to his friends Niall Montgomery and Niall Sheridan, to his agents at A. M. Heath, Patience Ross and Mark Hamilton, and to his new publisher during the 1960s, Timothy O'Keeffe, reveal that these novels are intended as vigorous textual experiments. In *The Hard Life*, O'Brien works with readily recognized fictional patterns in order to dismantle them. Masquerading as a tame, straightforward novel, *The Hard Life* explores the oblique ways silences are referred to by insufficient substitutes. As an "exegesis of squalor," it attempts to show the way, to secure coherence, to compensate for a lack of meaning behind words. Ironically, the text exposes how disordered incompleteness, which talk tries to counteract, becomes more troubling and intriguing with each effort of verbal intercourse.

The most significant features of *The Dalkey Archive* stem from O'Brien's late and surprising shift to a third-person point of view. As late as 6 January 1964, O'Brien radically altered the major thrust of the novel. The former "protagonist," Mick Shaugh-nessey, was significantly demoted, and O'Brien began developing a new third-person narrator as a most provocative storytelling sensibility. Through this new histrionic narrator, O'Brien scoffs at the disposition of novels to revolve around character, determining predictable paths limited by spent serial arrangements. By fatuously conforming to conventional formats, *The Dalkey Archive* powerfully implodes continuity, development, and literary redemption. Instead of pushing through boundaries of fiction, this novel yanks them out of shape through its gravitational parodies.

Flann O'Brien's
Exorbitant Novels

1

Comhthrom Feinne and *Blather:* The Early Experiments

—The schoolmen were schoolboys first, Stephen said super-
politely. Aristotle was once Plato's schoolboy.
                                                    —*Ulysses*

Long thunderstorms, like those which interrupt late summer
afternoons and crash on through the night, are often deceptive.
The average thunderstorm has a lifespan of only fifty-five minutes. What seems to us an extended climatic event is usually a
series of brief storms, one prompting another: "When the conditions are right a pod will be forming in the area as the older pod is
dissipating its energies. Thus we get the impression of one single
storm lasting for hours. Not so."[1] Structurally, Flann O'Brien's
first novel, *At Swim-Two-Birds*, proves as illusive as these extensive
environmental eruptions. While the student-narrator's progress
through the university fakes a traditional continuity, the novel is
more properly viewed as a series of improvisations, each with a
distinct, provocative, local coherence. The self-conscious fracturing of narrative "progress" is purposeful, intended to challenge
our learned means of making shape. But the repetitive rupturing
attests to a practical imperative as well as to a theoretical concern.
In his literary compositions prior to *At Swim*, O'Brien became
more adept at creating scenes than he was at constructing an
extended narrative. As the author of articles and essays for University College, Dublin's *Comhthrom Feinne* and as founder, editor,
and author of his own magazine, *Blather*, he developed a flair for
brief, highly charged, parodic "pods." An examination of these
early creative efforts significantly enhances our appreciation of
O'Brien as novelist. Although his university publications are inconsistent in quality, the best reveal many of the characteristic
impulses which inform his subsequent fictions.

17

To date, O'Brien's early writing career has not received adequate critical attention.[2] The literary inventions composed between 1931 and 1934 deserve careful consideration because they clearly and vitally enhance our understanding of Brian O'Nolan as the novelist Flann O'Brien. On even a surface level, many of these early fictions manifest his inclination toward imaginative subversion, his penchant for parody, and his self-conscious consideration of style as performance. Only slightly beneath their casualness and wit, we hear a lively, questioning author probing what will become crucial critical propositions about the activity of writing.

In 1931, at the age of nineteen, O'Brien made his literary debut in the UCD student magazine, *Comhthrom Feinne*. He continued to write for and occasionally edit this publication until 1935, when he brought out his own magazine, *Blather.* During these years, his extravagant performances were anxiously anticipated and highly appreciated by contemporaries such as Niall Sheridan, Cyril Cusack, Sean O'Faolain, Niall Montgomery, and Donagh MacDonagh. From the outset, O'Brien began to make a (few) name(s) for himself and is remembered as an unpredictable, eccentric, and unfailingly exciting writer. The April 1934 issue pays him this homage: "He was, under various pseudonyms, particularly that of Brother Barnabas, the most successful and popular contributor *Comhthrom Feinne* has ever had" (*CF* VIII.1.23).[3] Although O'Brien occasionally signed articles with his real name or initials, Brian O'Nolan, Brian Ua Nuallain, B. O'N., or B. Ua N., he frequently masked himself behind diverse pen names. In the first anniversary issue of *Comhthrom Feinne*, the editor remarks: "We have seen some very good sketches over the names of . . . Mr. B. Ua Nuallain, who persisted in hiding his light under a bushel by using initials other than his own" (*CF* IV.2.217). Niall Montgomery recalls O'Brien's debut at UCD as auspicious and characteristically subversive. He is said to have descended, "like a shower of paratroopers, deploying a myriad of pseudonymous personalities in the interest of pure destruction."[4] From the outset of his literary career, O'Brien is particularly wary of establishing any predictable, stable "identity" in language. He employs multiple pseudonyms in *Comhthrom Feinne* and *Blather,* as he will throughout his career, because he is always uneasy with the precarious nature of any "self" constructed through words. The flair for satire, the interest in literary "destruction," and the need to mask himself are all characteristic authorial traits developed prior to the invention of *At Swim-Two-Birds*.

Between May 1931 and May 1934, Brother Barnabas constructs himself in piecemeal fashion as a salacious savant with an impossibly expansive life. Born "a halfcaste Russian Jew . . . of good *kulak* stock," he single-handedly dissolves a Danish Reichstag in 1887. In 1912, "responsible for a tiny but gilded principality in the wilds of the Siberian Steppes," he finds time to "dog whip . . . Der Grosse Kaiser Wilhelm" in Vienna. Later, acting as detective, he happens upon Fludd and Bernard Shaw living incognito "for two days in Loreto Hall disguised as two little girls dressed in blue." He also, more suggestively, "discovered and hastily recovered James Joyce" (*CF* VI.3.47 and 65). By 1933, although quite old, he is beset by

> teething, whooping cough, mumps, rickets, and a host of other infantile complaints. . . . He is attended day and night by a buxom nurse provided by the Board of Works, and the giggles and hoarse chuckling that can be heard at dusk from the density of the turf-trollops bespeak a waggish vitality that is reluctant to yield the palm to Father Time. (*CF* VI.3.47)

Appearing in only five issues of *Blather* from August 1934 to January 1935, the persona of Count O'Blather is nevertheless just as fantastically fishy. The Count is a self-proclaimed "publicist, playwright, poet, politician, and press-baron" as well as the author of the compelling pamphlet "The O'Blather Attitude on Ping Pong." Relentless proponent of constructing a major Atlantic port at Bettystown, inventor of "Patent Woollen Panties [which] say good-bye to colds," the O'Blather, as we shall see, also earns a reputation as the most eclectic, ubiquitous sportsman of any day (*B* I.5.92 and I.1.3).[5]

The creation of these character/authors attests to O'Brien's flair for "posing," an activity of which he enjoys taking advantage. In *At Swim*, authors are treated as "things" to be created so that "they" (the student narrator, Trellis, Tracy, Orlick, Shanahan, Furriskey, and Lamont) might fabricate other presences and predicaments. The narrator of *The Third Policeman*, ingeniously deprived of his name, shares a problematic predilection with O'Brien:

> "I was once acquainted with a tall man," he [Sergeant Pluck] said to me at last, "that had no name either and you are certain to be his son and the heir to his nullity and all his nothings. What way is your pop today and where is he?"
> It was not, I thought, entirely unreasonable that the son of a man who had no name should have no name also but it was clear that the

Sergeant was confusing me with somebody else. This was no harm and I decided to encourage him. I considered it desirable that he should know nothing about me but it was even better if he knew several things which were quite wrong. . . .
"He is gone to America," I replied. (*TP* 56–57)[6]

Employing a variety of masks, O'Brien continually experiments with constructing a "self" through the activity of writing. In the early posings especially, we see an acute self-consciousness as "author" expressed through parodies of literary and nonliterary conventions. He takes pains to keep authorial identity floating or in flux to resist becoming reified or static. At its most interesting, putting pen to paper becomes for O'Brien a contest between protecting and endangering an invented self. And in the context of always giving us a show, he locates and explores agitating, inherent constraints of writing against which he enthusiastically pushes.

Brother Barnabas is first heard from in the second issue of *Comhthrom Feinne*, 15 May 1931, with a preposterous article, "The 'L and H' from the Earliest Times." The ostensible occasion for this piece is the defense of UCD's Literary and Historical Society from the "broadside vocalism of the obstructionist, and the more insidious attacks of the non-believer from without the fold" (*CF* I.2.31). To confirm the reputation of The Literary and Historical Society, Brother Barnabas locates its "authority" in tangible texts "unconscionably ancient." The obvious idiom of the religious reactionary then modulates into the style of self-conscious literary editor:

> Accordingly, all excerpts printed below should be committed to memory, care being taken when reciting them, to pronounce all proper names with the slight sing-song intonation current in the latter part of the Stone Age. These excerpts are compiled from the original Minutes which stretch back far beyond the Palaeolithic Age. All the spellings have been modernised, and the texts have been extensively revised with a view to the Amendment (Censorship of Publications) Act. (*CF* I.2.31–32)

Progressing from the days of dinosaurs through the flub of Guy Fawkes, this "history," like O'Brien's first novel, repeatedly fractures itself as it questions semantic procedures which we routinely overlook in more traditional manuscripts.

Date . . .*

Curious semi-legible references to "members' tails." Chairman "takes the bough." Debate is illegible. Auditor unknown.

Date . . .

Auditor reads several stones on the interesting subject, "Is Civilization a Failure?" Subsequent motion to build a home for decayed ex-auditors with the manuscript is rejected on humanitarian grounds.

Date . . .

Member ejected for cracking a joke "in the worst possible taste" during private business.† Insistent non-member, Mr. Yhaclum, has his tail pulled and is ejected. Egg of dinosaur thrown by disapproving bystander. Debate and further proceedings illegible.

Date . . .

New auditor, Mr. Tnek. Is suspected of having glass eyes, as he continues to fix one part of the house with a gaze of unnatural dog-like devotion, or alternatively, a glare of fanatical fish-like hatred. He takes things quietly.‡ Delivers Inaugural Address with tail exposed and wagging nervously.§ Makes an unexpected witty retort toward the end of his auditorship, and is burnt on a pyre of crude paraffin wax.

The Minutes for several centuries subsequently have been irreparably damaged by Phoenician settlers, who have used the stones for the sharpening of bronze weapons. One curious word, "Neoinín-clog," is still plainly legible on many slabs. It is probably the Erse title of a pagan love saga, a double-cycle of which is known to have existed.

The next legible set of Minutes, in a much better condition, are scratched on stout elephant hide.

Date A.D. 198.

Auditor, Mr. F. McCool, B.Agr. Sc. Mr. McCool, speaking first in Irish and continuing in English, said he wished to draw the attention of members to a reference in the Minutes of previous—very previous—meetings to "members' tails." Speaking for himself, he did not like it. These Minutes, unless they were altered or destroyed, would remain to embarrass and humiliate the members of the future, the

---

*Parts of the Minutes here are illegible, owing to the vandalism of Erse writers several centuries later, who covered the granite Minute-stones with crude "Ogham" notchings.

†Curiously enough, this joke will appear singularly innocuous to the modern mind: It runs: Why is a bud like a sud? Because one raps the batto and the other baps the ratto!

‡This is ambiguous, perhaps deliberately so.

§This is obviously the origin of the present beautiful custom of delivering the Inaugural Address in "tails," a custom which has been revered and respected by the gentleman Auditor throughout the ages.

members of generations still unborn; more especially those who aspire to match supremacy of intellect with dignity of carriage. He therefore proposed that all incriminating Minutes be dumped in the sea at Dollymont (now Dollymount), where a mammoth skating rink could be constructed. Speaking then, in his official capacity, he had no hesitation in accepting the motion.*

Mr. Yaf, B.Naut.Sc., who was suspected to be a Viking, and spoke with a curious foreign accent, said he was interested in international peace, and he wished to object. To place *all* the incriminating Minutes in the sea would lead to a phenomenal increase in coastal erosion all over the world. To the best of his recollection, he had never met the word "skating" or "rink" in any of the many books he had read, and was therefore reluctantly compelled to condemn the thing or the practice, or whatever it was. He courteously thanked the house.

The further excerpts transcribed include an address by "Mr. Oisin, D.Litt.Celt.," who speaks "in metres too intricate to be recorded" and one by "Henry VIII Deo Grat. Rex, a chieftain from a neighboring island" who debates the proposition "The more we are together, the happier we will be." Brother Barnabas then closes this history with the punning palaver of the party beneath the 1605 Gunpowder Plot:

> Several sets of Minutes, covering the gap between the foregoing and the next available notes, which are inscribed on fossilised goatskin, are in the course of being deciphered.
>
> **Date . . .**
> Auditor: Mr. G. R. Fawkes, B.Sc. Mr. Fawkes, in thanking the members for electing him, said he would endeavor to make the Society go with a bang. He had pleasure in nominating his friend, Mr. Tresham, to take his place during his temporary absence in London. He was going to attend an Inter-debate at Westminster, the mother of Parliaments, *muryaa,* and they could bet he would be at the bottom of a very far-reaching motion there. He would ask the gentlemen at the door to stop letting off squibs; his nerves were bad enough, God knows.
>
> Strangely enough, there is no trace of an Inaugural Address by Mr. Fawkes. (*CF* I.2.31–32)

For all its schoolboy humor, this article presents the first indication of O'Brien's interest in texts as substantial artifacts, tangible

---

*This extraordinary breach of procedure demonstrates the antiquity of the vice of flaunting the constitution and all rules of debate, so frequently the last refuge of the half-wit Auditor throughout the ages.

areas which invite and interact with the imposition of signs. Since the "original Minutes" are transcribed on stone slabs, the texts might conveniently double as raw material for the construction of "a home for decayed ex-auditors." Later, in an inadvertent act of literary "deconstruction," Phoenician settlers abuse these monolithic manuscripts, employing them as whetting agents for their newfangled bronze weapons. And Finn MacCool, most like O'Brien, desires to utilize the texts as an "arena" for play. He proposes that previous Minutes, which could prove embarrassing, be used to construct a mammoth skating rink. Never mind that a "skating rink" cannot be built until the words "skating" and "rink" appear in books, authorizing "the thing or the practice or whatever . . . ." Presumably, the term "mausoleum" could not replace the phrase "home for decayed ex-auditors" since the tomb of Mausolos at Halicarnassus, dating from about 350 B.C., had not yet been built. Logically, the substitution of "stout elephant hide" for granite, as a material on which to inscribe signs, enables the pun on "mammoth skating rink." And the Phoenicians' textual "erasures" further complicate prior acts of palimpsest when Erse writers vandalised several sets of ancient Minutes, covering "the granite Minute-stones with crude 'Ogham' notchings." "Vandalism" would be allowed since the term is supplied by Brother Barnabus centuries after the Germanic Vandals overran Europe and sacked Rome in 455 A.D.

Focusing on these bizarre, yet naturally sensible, types of manuscripts, O'Brien deliberately jars his readers from any casual response to the all too familiar forms of ink and paper. He prompts us to consider that the seemingly "natural" procedures of more typical volumes may be viewed as just as arbitrary, yet just as full of wild possibilities. One set of minutes often prompts or *begets* future writings whether in the form of subsequent minutes which refer back to prior texts or subsequent footnotes which seem to add credibility to the "primary" writings. This interest in *writing over* prior writings becomes a labyrinthine enterprise in *At Swim* where readers are meant to enjoy getting intriguingly lost in networks of palimpsests. And the play with critical footnotes anticipates the extended and consequential performance in *The Third Policeman*, in which the notes can outdistance the supposed primary inscriptions of a chapter.

It is precisely this view of texts as corporeal entities which elicits some of O'Brien's most imaginative and theoretically intriguing writing. In later issues of *Comhthrom Feinne*, one Lionel Prune, modeled after W. B. Yeats, threatens to upstage Brother Barnabas as the leading poet of the day. The irate cleric answers the charge of the "journeyman dilletante," finding pretext for assault in the diaphanous character of the magazine's sheeting:

> In the ordinary course of events (writes Brother Barnabas), an outrage on good-taste on the part of the editorial staff of *Comhthrom Feinne* might be condoned on the extenuating grounds of youth and inexperience, and the present writer would not be the last to turn the blind eye, and to afford the youthful sinners the charity of silence. When, however, he finds that this outrage has been printed on the back of a page bearing a composition of his own, and realising that the composition of his own is separated from this Literary abortion by approximately one thousandth part of an inch, then duty to self and country must brush aside all trivial considerations of etiquette. (*CF* IV.2.226)

A fanciful, extended controversy ensues with each author displaying parodic "real poetry" and satiric examples of "modern" literary criticism. The attacks on modernity and the latest literary theories are the consequence of too close quarters. Through the pellucid quality of the paper, Brother Barnabas finds his "presence" rubbed the wrong way by Prune's.

In later years, masked as the journalist Myles na Gopaleen, O'Brien comically calls attentions to the ways the construct of a page and our left-to-right, top-to-bottom procedures of reading inform what can be written. Throughout his novelistic career—from *At Swim-Two-Birds* through *The Dalkey Archive*—he exhibits an amplified awareness of how local textual properties influence the ways words (or any other signs) might mean. This example, from the pages of the *Irish Times*, requires precise spacing:

> On a recent Thursday I went to the pictures and saw a tall gentleman called Randolph Scott in a film called "The Spoilers." At the end of the picture Randolph gets into a fight with another man in a pub.

At the end of the fight there is no pub. The fight is so fierce that it is reduced to smithereens. Randolph, being the bad lot, gets a frightful thrashing, a frtfull throshou, a frajfyl tromaking, a fruitful . . .

The Plain People of Ireland: Whatsamatter?

Myself: Feel queer . . . dark . . . nase blooding . . . giddy . . . where am I?

The Plain People of Ireland: Ah sure you often meet that in the pictures, too—that's altitude. You're too high up. No oxygen. The pilots do often have a black out. Come on down lower in the page and you'll be game ball.

Myself: All right. Thanks.

The Plain People of Ireland: Are you OK now?

Myself: Yes, thanks, I'm feeling all right now. Well, as I was saying, Randolph gets a frightful hiding, he is a terrible mess when the picture ends. But the following night I happen to see the same Randolph in another picture called, I think, "The Texan." All I can say is, fit and well he was looking after the hammering he got the night before.

The Plain People of Ireland: Will you have a bit of sense man. "The Texan" is an old picture. A real ould stager man. But "The Spoilers" is a new picture. It doesn't say because you see the one on wan night and then d'other on another—

Myself: Say no more. I realise I have been hasty. I will think before I shoot my mouth off next time.

Yes. Let me see. Not bad down here. Sort of . . . cool. The daddy was a steeplejack but I was never a man for heights. Though many's a time I bought an irish-timesful of chips from that Italian chap Vertigo.[7]

Considering *Comhthrom Feinne* as O'Brien's basic training in these matters, we can reexamine the footnotes Brother Barnabas concocts for his first "L and H" article. It is an old game, played masterfully by Laurence Sterne in *Tristram Shandy* and subsequently finessed by O'Brien in *The Third Policeman*. In the "L and H" pseudohistory, Brother Barnabas's footnotes confirm his probing of the ways a text—any text—invites and enables subtexts with their own peculiar processes. Each footnote offers itself as an "extraordinary breach of procedure"; the reader glances down to the bottom of the page, interrupting the horizontal progress of one's eyes, fracturing the sequential, linear relationships between words which govern most texts. As breaches, the footnotes may be seen as indicative of the narrative rupturing for which *At Swim*, like *Tristram Shandy*, is famous.

While some of the footnotes are frivolous (and deliberately so), the first two deserve some scrutiny. The first note ostensibly accounts for the brevity and imprecision of the Paleolithic excerpts. In his role as scholar, Brother Barnabas explains how subsequent "writers" violated the earliest Minutes by superimposing their own text over the "original." The introduction of the "Ogham" script reinforces the focus on textual tangibility while it also introduces one of O'Brien's obsessive concerns—the nature of palimpsest.

Ogham is a system of writing which flourished in Ireland between the fourth and seventh centuries A.D. The Ogham alphabet is composed of fifteen consonant symbols—lines touching or crossing a stone edge—and five vowel symbols—round notches on the edge. Individual characters are arranged in patterns running vertically up rough standing stone. Letters, words, and combinations of words are determined by the shape of, and distance between, impressions. Some of the signs, such as the examples below, might remind one of morse code transcribed for the hard of hearing:

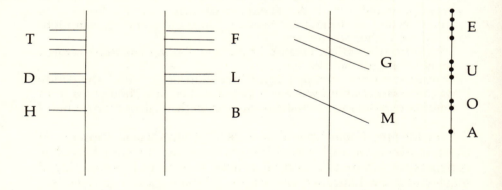

The Brother's first footnote prompts us to consider, abstractly and theoretically, how the peculiarities of such a system of discourse shape the act of telling. Obviously, the ancient scribe would have to find stone with a texture soft enough to scratch yet hard enough to sustain or preserve an imprint. The stone slab would also need a sharp edge to serve as a reference point for the characters. Employing six fewer consonants and proceeding from bottom to top, the Ogham system accentuates the ways textual idiosyncrasies necessarily inform what may be said.

In many of these early pieces, O'Brien looks into the activities of writing as willful events. The continuing concern which animates his writing is a skepticism of an author's ability to beget. He seems to seek out obstacles and occasions to test the degree to which either tangible textual dictates or covert rules of discourse may usurp the authority of the writer. O'Brien energetically explores, as Michel Foucault has more recently, the extent to which an author employs language and the extent to which he is the employee of language.

The "vandalism" of the Erse writers also suggests O'Brien's budding interest in the nature of textual palimpsest. He stresses the activity of writing by emphasizing the way a text often, intentionally, superimposes itself over previous writing. The Ogham notchings cover over and partially displace the "original" Minutes producing a peculiar effect in which *At Swim* repeatedly participates. The student narrator is constantly writing over (not revising) his "spare-time literary activities," fortuitously enabling Orlick to "re-create" Finn's rendition of Mad Sweeny, while Furriskey, Shanahan, and Lamont place their version of Trellis's tortures over Orlick's prior mutinous manuscript. In O'Brien's fiction, the passages most worth noticing are those in which a style or structure previously shaped in words shows through a passage we are presently reading.

Of imminent interest are the degrees to which the erasure or eradication of writing is possible *through* writing. Such modern critical questions are rescued from becoming "issues," however, by the sportive playfulness with which O'Brien raises them. Finn MacCool subtly alludes to such problematics when he jauntily suggests eradicating incriminating evidence by constructing a skating rink from the stone Minutes. For O'Brien, palimpsest is less a matter of eradication than it is an opportunity for creative distortion. His superimposition of texts is more like a moire effect where one wavy design *covers* another at an angle, producing a pattern distinct from its components. The excitement of such deliberate distortion issues from the tension of constructing a new text by violating an antecedant.

The "singularly innocuous joke" of the second footnote ("Why is a bud like a sud? Because one raps the batto and the other baps the ratto") is meant to provoke our urge to solve linguistic riddles. It is a clever conundrum, luxuriating in rhythm, rhyme, and witty reversals of spoonerism. With a little help from Eric Partridge one can, if one so desires, arrive at a "solution." Consider "bud" as a small child, and "sud" as suds, beer. "Raps" is the act of swearing against, providing damaging witness, and "baps" is short for baptize, a traditional dunking punishment for the pickpocket. "Batto" is slang for bat, a prostitute preferring night duty; "ratto" is old colloquial Scottish for rat. Solving then for variable x: A child bears witness against a whore; the fruit of her labor is evidence of her illicit pleasures. In a "similar" way, sud is the agent which testifies to a rat's crime; a larcenous rodent often baptizes himself, floundering and foundering amidst the beer vat from which he sampled.

Perhaps.

The joke is on us, however, if we take too seriously our desire to make it *mean*. The riddle seems to me essentially a collection of nonsense sounds to be enjoyed by the audial imagination. O'Brien is sounding out one of the primary fields of discourse, testing the ground to see how much it gives. As an inquisitive craftsman, he investigates the aural experience of syllables, words, or sentence sounds as potentially separable from their "normal" meaning determined through conceptual decoding. O'Brien shares with Viktor Shklovsky—but without any "debt" to Russian Formalism—a persistent urge to make language "strange" to us, to reinvigorate our overly familiar relationship with words. Never satisfied with words as fixed objects with stable references, he feels free to lop off letters, rearrange them, and form new, perhaps "illegal" signs. We see this same healthy disrespect for traditional networks of coherence when the student narrator of *At Swim* distorts Laocoon's famous warning about the Trojan horse as he innovatively constructs "two decadent Greek scullions, Timothy Danaos and Dona Ferentes" (*AS* 142).[8] O'Brien's urge to run interference between the sound image and concept of a sign produces much of the subversive inversion on which his novels thrive.

The exercise of the bud/sud joke is as innocent and interesting as the punning of the first excerpt, with its references to "members' tails" and the chairman "taking the bough." The fun depends on the instability of the reference. The degree of divergence between "bending from the waist in formal attire" and "climbing trees assisted by a primitive appendage" is temporarily collapsed by the identity of the sound image "bou." A fine line separates being merely clever with words and prompting an interesting attention to semantic operations. I am arguing that O'Brien's subversive humor proves theoretically precocious; his satiric comedies often anticipate postmodern considerations of linguistic properties and processes.

Having successfully established himself as an historical authority, Brother Barnabas decides to try on the robes of oracle. The opening number of the succeeding year (29 January 1932) includes "The Brother Barnabas College Almanac" which offers the following suggestive prognostications:

Brother Barnabas, who has left Baden-Baden and gone to Carlsbad for the waters, gives to each one of his lady readers a Saccharine Platonic kiss, a thousand times sweeter than its name, and to his gentlemen readers he bows courteously and cordially, but from a distance; to the Auditors and their assistant officers, the Staff of our Academic Life, Patient Dustmen of Life's Garbage-waggon, Sweet Cigarettes to our Nicotine-craving Lungs, Corpse-washers in Life's Mortuary, Blessed beans of the gods, he extends his brotherly bonhomie, rich as treacle, a condiment that will sweeten the sourest Academic Pudding. To All and All, his blessing in the dawn of a new and unprecedented year. To the young in particular, he gives a strong exhortation to spend a twelvemonth of sober unremitted toil, that Old Age may not find them with one foot in the grave and the other upon the bottomest rung of the Ladder of Success; to the old and grey and feeble he recommends his own invaluable monograph: "Inveterate Drunkards Cured In a Week by Patent Painless Secret Method, together with a Supplement treating of the Deterioration of Tissue Consequent upon Inordinate Alcoholic Inebriation.". . .

January 8.—Will fall on a Friday. Term re-opens. Ryan suddenly discovers that January is the month of Janus, dedicated to Hall-porters and decides to make himself a votive offering; decides not to make a beast of himself and gives Jimmy a sup. . . .

January 23.—America declares war on Japan . . . ; Brother Barnabas pares his corns. . . .

April 5.—College re-opens.

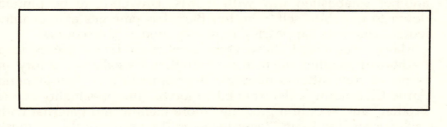

The above is a portrait of himself presented to the College by Brother Barnabas, depicting himself walking through a snow storm from Baden-Baden to Carlsbad, clad in white pyjamas, followed by a flock of white ponies. Overhead, as if leading the way, is a mystic white guillemot. Meeting of the Governing Body called to discuss the Gift.

April 16.—Cash betting between Students, Hall-porters and Professors in the Billiard-room, banned by the S.R.C. on the grounds that it might "lead Students to forget their dignity." Three Professors gallantly decide to stake their degrees on their play. . . .

> *May 29.*—10,000 beds arrive together with 600 tons of bedding.
>
> . . . .
>
> (These dots denote the passage of the carefree Summer holidays, spent by many in the kindly company of their books.)
>
> *October 15.*—College re-opens. Second Mammoth Billiard Tournament announced between "Professors and Non-professors," the former staking their degrees to a man. To be run off in 200 heats. Referee: the Hon. the Lord Mayor. . . .
>
> *December 15.*—Results of the Billiard Tournament announced: the following are the names of the winners with their newly acquired titles: Mick Ryan, F.R.S. D.Sc.; James Redmond, M.D., LL.D.; . . . B. O'Nuallain, E. Roarty, 25 B. Comms. each. New and distinguished looking Hall-porters take up duties. Term closes. Brother Barnabas suffers from a slight hiccup, but recovers sufficiently to take his usual afternoon walk. (*CF* III.1.146–47)

Many of the local references here correlate thematically with O'Brien's novels. The billiard tournament (in which O'Nolan wins 25 B. Comms.), for instance, participates in the decadent undergraduate profile further developed in *At Swim*. And the "invaluable monograph," designed to assist habitual boozers, smacks of the brother's self-help, mail-order schemes so prominent in *The Hard Life*. But these early articles interest me more as indications of O'Brien's turn for theoretic examination. One primary consideration is the way Brother Barnabas flaunts his verbal dexterity, parodying a variety of styles. Each time we meet him, he spoofs another established way with words. Unwilling to be pinned down to a stable "self," Brother Barnabas emerges as a chameleonic "character" appearing in motley modes of discourse.

Many critics read these early *Comhthrom Feinne* pieces in a traditional manner, focusing on Brother Barnabas's identity in terms of conventional narrative development and denouement. Anne Clissmann is determined to locate "the personality of the Brother" and sees him growing "more mellow and paternal with each succeeding issue."[9] Her focus on the events of the Brother's "life" disposes her to accommodate him to a familiar pattern. She claims that: "Just as Brother Barnabas had reached [the] height of power, influence and indeed, almost god-like omniscience, the classic, tragic fall came."[10] For O'Brien, however, the only significant "events" are those which occur in and through a style; he demonstrates little concern for consistently developing a personality for his pseudonym. As a construct, Brother Barnabas provides occasions for trying out types of talk, testing their resiliency through parody. While prophesying (in 1932) that America will declare war on Japan, "Brother Barnabas pares his corns," playing the role of Stephen Dedalus's "God of the creation" who, in *A Portrait*, remains "indifferent, paring his fingernails."[11] Yet O'Brien never intends to place Brother Barnabas in the position of that imagined god, "beyond or above his handiwork, invisible, refined out of existence."[12] More like Neptune's herdsman Proteus, O'Brien prides himself on the display of the Brother's plastic shapings.

In this instance, the Brother seems determined to literalize linguistically the geographic relationship between Carlsbad and Dublin. Everything about the introduction assures that author and audience maintain a decorous distance, their separation achieved through the fashion of the address. The Brother begins almost beyond "himself" speaking of himself in the third person, as if an intruding editorial sensibility filtered the cleric's greeting to his flock of readers. He then dusts off a select vocabulary and paced-off, protracted sentence structures which affect a passé appearance. We listen to the deft combination of a formally mannered salutation ("to each one of his lady readers . . . to the Auditors and their assistant officers . . . To All and All . . ."), overly solicitous alliterations ("courteously and cordially," "brotherly bonhomie"), and a parodic listing of heroic compliments ("Staff of our Academic Life, Patient Dustmen of Life's Garbage-waggon, Sweet Cigarettes to our Nicotine-craving Lungs, Corpse-washers in Life's Mortuary, Blessed beans of the gods"). Such an address mixes a cloyingly sweet concoction which calls for dilution by more than the Carlsbad spa's waters.

If this salaaming were just one more mask of the Brother's, the performance might remain merely amusing. But an authorial self-consciousness of himself as "player" and his enthusiasm for striking attitudes in language fundamentally inform the charge and packing of O'Brien's novels. As in *At Swim* and *The Third Policeman*, this extraordinary, extravagant verbal posturing makes demands of the reader which prompt consideration of the exciting problematics of language.

In a subtle, almost ancillary way, the address explores the nature of signs and the covert codes which influence their interaction. The reader might consider, for instance, the phrase "Saccharine Platonic kiss, a thousand times sweeter than its name." Although introduced in a casual manner, the reference attests to one of O'Brien's motivating passions—the investigation of disparity between "word" and "thing." How sweet is his Saccharine Platonic kiss? "Saccharin" names a white, crystalline powder with a molecular formula ($C_7H_5 NO_3S$) whose sweetness is supposedly equivalent to five hundred times that of cane sugar. Since this display of affection is "a thousand times sweeter than its name," we arrive at a platonic kiss approximately five hundred thousand times sweeter than sucrose granules. However, mathematics—as one system of knowing—is not our concern here. Brother Barnabas's curious hyperbole incites a consideration of the nature of metaphor, how language necessarily refers to itself, and questions the precariousness of any effort to name.

Admittedly, it is easy, once one gets going, to make too much of this "queer stuff," flirting with the boundaries of mental ludo. But I am especially intrigued with the way O'Brien's writing engages us in colloquy, urging the reader to converse with the words on the page. For me, it is enough that such theoretical questions are raised; pursuing the question is always more vital than arriving at an answer. Like Shanahan in *At Swim*, we are prompted to "prefer the question to the answer. It serves . . . us as a bottomless pretext for scholarly dialectic" (*AS* 274).

In this context, it is worthwhile reexamining the procession of heroic compliments which serve the Auditors and their assistants: "the Staff of our Academic Life, Patient Dustmen of Life's Garbage-waggon, Sweet Cigarettes to our Nicotine-craving Lungs, Corpse-washers in Life's Mortuary, Blessed beans of the gods." This series spotlights inventive metaphor, but it also serves as an occasion for maneuvers in language similar to those of *At Swim's* "Memorandum of the respective diacritical traits or qualities of Messrs. Furriskey, Lamont and Shanahan" (*AS* 231–32). In both cases, O'Brien negotiates with the usual temporal procedures which dictate that saying one thing necessarily precludes saying something else at that time. The protracted length of the Brother's opening sentence stresses how we read and speak horizontally through time, establishing meaning in terms of sequential relationships. The heroic compliments, however, partially wrest the reader's headway; like a twist of the Pooka's magic thumb, they cause a "stasis of the natural order and a surprising kinesis of many incalculable influences hitherto in suspense" (*AS* 252). The metaphors ascribed to the Auditors almost postpone the forward movement of the sentence. Our immediate attention is focused on the way a word is also defined vertically, now, by its difference from a range of "suspended" words which might have been, but were not, chosen at that time. Brother Barnabas chooses to address the Auditors as "Patient Dustmen of Life's Garbage-waggon," but he simultaneously desires to avoid deferring other terms such as "Sweet Cigarettes to our Nicotine-craving Lungs" and "Corpse-washers in Life's Mortuary." His phrasings deliberately and provocatively call attention to the fundamental competitions between horizontal and vertical or diachronic and synchronic linguistic procedures. O'Brien's subsequent novels thrive on such turns, repeatedly sounding the ways any linguistic system refers not so much to a reality beyond, as to its own enabling processes.

This interest in the disposition of signs similarly informs the supercilious explanation of dots denoting "the passage of the carefree Summer holidays" as well as the picture of Brother Barnabas trekking between Baden-Baden and Carlsbad. At this time, another look at the portrait is warranted:

April 5.—College re-opens.

The above is a portrait of himself presented to the College by Brother Barnabas, depicting himself walking through a snow storm from Baden-Baden to Carlsbad, clad in white pyjamas, followed by a flock of white ponies. Overhead, as if leading the way, is a mystic white guillemot. Meeting of the Governing Body called to discuss the Gift. (*CF* III.1.146–47)

The blank picture of white objects seen through snow is an old gag, but Brother Barnabas transcends the mere tradition through his museum-label, "fine art" vocabulary. We are told that the Brother is there, clad in white pj's, making his way through a snow storm. For better measure, he is accompanied by albino ponies and winged sea fowl similarly devoid of pigment. The absurd portrait gently plays with the precarious relationship between naming and presence. Since "X", in order to be identified as "X," must be distinguishable from "W" and "Y," our visual attention is redirected from the uniformly bleached field of the portrait to the black border lines which "frame" the cleric and his cohorts. By extension, the game calls into question the volatile ways words operate on a page. In this context, O'Brien anticipates theorists such as Jacques Derrida, prompting us to explore how the difference between signs and their *différance* from other possible substitutes essentially determine the presence to which words aspire.

In March 1933, Brother Barnabas presents one of the most outlandish and intriguing abuses of signs in his scholastic *coup de théâtre*, *"AN CONGAR"*:

What is AN CONGAR? Briefly, it is the short-cut to the mastery of the Irish Language, and is guaranteed to be shorter than any previous short-cut by at least 80 miles, 7 roods and 2 perches, Irish Bog Measure. It eliminates Syntax, abolishes Idiom and annihilates Vocabulary; it reduces the Irish Language down to simple mathematical symbols; it obviates drudgery; it does away with old-fashioned textbooks and will enable the persecuted inhabitants of West Cork to face the attentions of fanatic Oleryites with the courage and the hope that scientific knowledge alone can give. Ni beag sin, or *xyz*. (*CF* V.3.48)

This quick and easy method claims to make Irish available to anyone with "A KNOWLEDGE OF ELEMENTARY MATHEMATICS and a reasonable amount of faith in human nature" (*CF* V.3.48). By distorting the authorized systems of algebra, geometry, and trigonometry, the Brother's project investigates "the content of Gaelic words."

One provocative Congar is a send-up of the family, friends, and intended career of Vivion de Valera, a fellow student of O'Brien's at UCD. Son of Eamon de Valera, prime minister of Ireland, Vivion opposed and defeated O'Brien for auditorship of the L and H a year earlier in 1932. O'Brien explains his version of their political rivalry in James Meenhan's *A Centenary History of the Literary and Historical Society of University College, Dublin, 1855–1955*. My focus, however, is not their rivalry but rather the way the Brother uses his foe's name to challenge networks of coherence and the properties of signs:

PROPOSITION III.—*Given that the Gaelic phrase Bheibheann de Bhalera = O, factorise Bheibheann de Bhalera.*

Everything must be a factor of itself and must contain at least one other extraneous and important quantity.   . . . .
. . . Axiom XVI.

For the purpose of argument, complete the square of de Bhalera.

Let y = the other unknown quantity.

Now, (Bheibheann de Bhalera)$^2 + y^2 = 0$.
But Bheibheann de Bhalaer = "Dev" ... ...
                                          Cainnt na nDaoine.

Therefore (Dev y) = 0.
    = Dev^2 + 2 Dev y + y^2 = 0.
But "Devy" is a diminutive form of "Dev" and means a small Dev or
young brother.
    Therefore Dev^2 + 2 (young brother) + y^2 = 0.
    Dev^2 + (Eamonn Rory) + y^2 = 0.
At this stage, the two young brothers may be taken out and sent
about their business for the time being.
    Then Dev^2 + y^2 = 0.
But y, being the other extraneous and important quantity, must
consist partly of politics.   ...   Deduction.
    Factorising y,
    Dev^2 + (Dáil)y = 0.
Allowing again for crudity of expression of AN CONGAR,
    Dev^2 + Dolly = 0.
Now bring in the two young brothers again.
    Then Dev^2 + 2 young brothers + Dolly = 0.
Factors of Bheibheann de Bhalera therefore are
    (Dev + eamonnagusruaidhri) (Dev + Dolly).
                                                    Q.E.F.

That is all to-day, children. (CF V.3.49)

This satiric implementation of the binomial theorem relies on
the perception of words and numbers as opaque, operative *things-
in-themselves* rather than as signifiers of signifieds beyond. At one
point, the expression "2 Dev y" is compressed into two "Devy"'s;
since a "Devy" is a small "Dev," we arrive at "2 (young brother)"
which is equivalent to "Eamonn Rory." Following Pascal's prescription for "expanding the binomial" (to which the proof is
remarkably faithful), the factorized middle term begets "eamonn-
agusruaidhri" by a process akin to the one which generates John
Furriskey of *At Swim*. Furriskey is "born" into the novel as a fully
formed adult by means of aestho-autogamy, "an operation involv-
ing neither fertilization nor conception," complicated solely by
"one unknown quantity on the male side" (*AS* 55).
    The formulaic, mathematical "proofs" of "An Congar" attest to
O'Brien's inclination to wreak havoc with all established systems
of coherence. Ironically, the precariousness of "paternal," logical
procedures, so conspicuous in this numerical satire, seem to remain covert once we switch to networks of words. O'Brien's
fictions make every effort to expose the ways similar procedures
inform and arbitrarily limit semantic artifacts from the process of a

sentence to the shape of a novel. De Selby's scientific proposals in *The Third Policeman* and the Pooka/Good Fairy dialogues of *At Swim* provide several examples of O'Brien's willingness to explore the absurd by gently modifying logical policies. The point, of course, is that the environments exposed seem "absurd" only because the genealogical customs of "reason" are considered normal. What saves all this from being worrisome or tedious is precisely the "modicum of unwonted levity" with which it is delivered (*TP* 94).

The preface of "An Congar" proves as sportively crazy as the scheme itself. The "unique System" is the product of Brother Barnabas's two-year epic adventure in "the depths of the Vatican Library" where, at one point, he "discovered in quick succession three separate values for the square root of a minus quantity before being overpowered by five able-bodied policemen." The chronicle of the Congar's completion is filled with "all-night struggles with refractory tangents, thrilling combats to the death with intransitive logarithms and veritable faction fights with swarms of subjunctive hypotenuses." The entire project was almost decimated by "a chance encounter with two Aorist Surds" who "appear to have originated in the darker years of the Middle Ages, and to have made their way through the Primitive Indian dialects, eventually arriving in Egypt about the year 1469." After transmigrating to the Aran Islands in the seventeenth century, they threaten the Brother's efforts in Rome but are eventually rebuffed "after 26 hours' stiff fighting" (*CF* V.3.48).

I have chosen the "Aorist Surd" nonsense because it offers great fun as well as a clue to the way O'Brien's mind maneuvers. The aorist verb tense in classical Greek denotes past action without indicating the completion of the action; an aorist experience is "indefinite" because its form provides no indication if or when the proceedings terminate. A mathematical *surd* is a sum composed of one or more irrational roots of numbers such as $\sqrt{2} + \sqrt{3}$; while in Gaelic *surd* is any willing and eager exertion, work undertaken with vigorous energy.

Like "aorist surds," O'Brien's fictions—especially his first two novels—accentuate the pleasures of vigorous exertion in the fields of incompletion and irrationality. In *At Swim*, the concourse of motley styles exposes the inability of any means of shaping to sustain itself in time. Repeatedly, one mode of expression displaces another, temporarily affirms its inherent shaping potency, but inevitably discloses its own inability to finish, to complete itself. Similarly, the dark comedy of *The Third Policeman* revolves around the indefinite circularity of the plot structure.

The narrator, a "poor misfortunate little bastard" who loses his name, faces the horror of an eternity of "unimaginable dimensions." He will repeatedly "return" to the crazy police station to face Sergeant Pluck's inevitable question: "Is it about a bicycle?" (*TP* 199). Yet the circle can never complete itself as each new revolution introduces an additional factor, fabricating still another "world of entirely new sensation and experience" (*TP* 95).

O'Brien's early undergraduate inventions often display his fascination with a verbal structure's proclivity for frustrating its own completion. A type of discourse proves "unsatisfactory" and therefore interesting, as it seems to arrest its suggested extension, allowing another way of forming to push against it and move off obliquely. One stylistic performance gives way to another temporarily deferred competitor, briefly affirming a precarious presence, while "closure" becomes an event relegated to an indefinite future. Two examples which bear most noticeably on the novels occur in *Blather* which O'Brien was putting together at the same time *At Swim* was taking shape.

The treatise "Rugby is Coming Back" purportedly rescinds a previous "lying ramp of last April [when] we wrote that Rugby was on the wane, that it was a spent force." As one might expect, *Blather* never even existed the previous April; its first edition appeared in August of 1934. The absence of the alleged antecedent article is a small matter, however, because at the present,

THE FACTS ARE THESE.

More and more people are going to play Rugby this season. More and more Gaels are going to take Dalkey trams to Croke Park. More and more tramps are going to croak in Dalkey gales, which no doubt means something in the lives of people who understand that sort of talk. (*B* I.3.54)

In the context of fabricating Blazes O'Blather's legendary career, the essay intriguingly "involves" itself, turning in on, and achieving form through, competing fields of discourse:

THE O'BLATHER WAS A GREAT SPORTSMAN

Like his distinguished father, Blazes O'Blather comes to the world of Irish sport with a great record and a fine family tradition. In the memorable Clontarf team which defeated England at Folkstone in 1912, The O'Blather combined brain and brawn in achieving a great victory. His position was behind the scrum, and opening with the Queen's Gambit, he sacrificed two pawns and managed to affect a very neat little mate with two bishops and a knight just as the final whistle was about to be blown. Playing faultless Rugby at Paris in the spring of the following year, he brought a clever French side to five sets before he would admit defeat, defeat which was in no small measure due to the fact that his hurley was smashed to atoms ten minutes before time, when victory was all but in sight.

A PROUD RECORD

In 1919 he joined Wanderers and formed the backbone of the team which visited Belgium in the autumn of the following year. The match was played on a Sunday in a downpour of rain, and though opposed to the cream of the Belgian clubs, the Irish team made a gallant and a worthy stand. The O'Blather, who had by this time acquired a considerable reputation for a safe pair of hands and a long kick, was in the front line of the forwards and opened up for Ireland with cue-ball in hand. Though faced with a particularly embarrassing double-baulk, he managed a cannon after employing no less than eighteen cushions. The clever if rather flukey manouvre left the red near the top cushion and the white on the centre spot. Two more cannons, four pots and a long jenny left the two balls properly "on" for the great break that was bound to ensue. Half-time score:—

Belgium, (rec. 1,000)   . . .   2,104.
The O'Blather, in play   . . .   2,558.

The rain became heavier at this point and Belgium apparently decided to vary their tactics. They cunningly introduced a slow bowler, evidently determined to make hay on the sodden pitch. The O'Blather, though busy with a series of peerless nursery cannons, quickly adjusted himself to the new threat and flogged the first over for three fours and four threes, cutting his drives through cover point and silly-mid-on with an abandon and a zest that would have done credit to a younger man. Three-quarter-time score:—

Belgium, (all out)   . . .   2,615.
The O'Blather   . . .   3,495. Unfinished

THE CLOSE OF AN EPIC STRUGGLE

Stumps and lots were drawn for tea at five-thirty when there were four inches of water on the pitch.

The same high standard of play was maintained on the resumption. The O'Blather had three strokes in hand and managed to half the sixteenth hole, thanks to some very neat work with his irons. Leading a fine handling movement, emanating from a scrum in midfield, he went over for a try at the seventeenth, thus putting Ireland farther in the lead and making the possibility of an equalising score even more remote.

From that moment the Irish team never looked back. And The O'Blather, playing faultless handball, obtained a solid in the last thirty seconds of the last minute and put the result beyond all doubt. (*B* I.3.54–55)

Throughout his careers as Brother Barnabas and Count O'Blather, O'Brien's ear for and attraction to "all sorts of talk" prompt and enable his most animated verbal performances. The accent here is on parody through discontinuity. Each unit of language, whether it be word, phrase, or sentence, misleads us by implying an extension which will give it an "acceptable" coherence and closure. Its genealogical proclivity is deliberately aborted, however, by playful disruption. The nostalgic history of The O'Blather's exploits is a head-faking romp through multiple conventions of sports reporting. Juxtaposing idiom, sentence structure, and scores from various athletic events, O'Brien concocts a fascinating mixture, imaginatively "coherent" in the dizzying manner of *At Swim*'s Circle N cowboy roundup.

The description of the 1912 match between Clontarf and England is a wild flight of fancy commencing on the field of rugby football, moving through strategies of chess, caroming off the cushions of billiards, pitching through cricket, chipping onto the greens of golf, finally arriving in the pit of Irish handball. By my count The O'Blather makes his way through at least eleven different activities here, some more than once.[13] Each improvisation has a local coherence which differs from and rebounds against the other sporting discourses which surround it. Like a talented rugby player going over for a try, O'Brien's language proceeds by feint, cut back, and deft passing of the give-and-go sort. Moving from one mode of expression to another, he sets up obstacles as he goes along, creating linguistic opponents to be dodged in getting from here to there.

Along the same lines, *Blather* got up a fabulous piece called "Hash" designed to circumvent the boring passages in novels as well as booksellers' rapaciousness. This is one volatile hodgepodge which ought to be savored from "beginning" to "end."

A novel—even a very bad one—can cost you a good sevenansixpence. Eleven or twelve novels can cost you *L*4 2*s.* 6*d.* (or *L*5 4*s.* 0*d.*, as the case may be). BLATHER, ever jealous for your honour and eager that you shall not let our grand old paper down by displays of ignorance or illiteracy when In Company, has pleasure in presenting the pith and the cream of eleven or twelve novels in the grand Nonstop Hash-up below.

You are saved the bother of wading through pages of muck in order to get at the good bits.

You must admit that we are a handy crowd of boys to have around the house. Write to us and thank us.

———————

Solitaire sat thoughtfully on a bunk in one of the cells of the jail that had been built in the back part of the sheriff's office. He realised that he was in a very difficult position. He was a prisoner in a town where he was an utter stranger.

I was a white man—the last product in the slow upward rise of mankind through the ages. I had to stop this thing if it cost me my life!

There was one way to do it—and the idea came to me so suddenly that I almost thought—well, never mind what I thought. I'm not ordinarily a religious man . . .

I could have done it before if I had only stopped to think instead of running. But now was another chance.

With a shriek that almost tore my lungs out, I leaped up on the stone.

A feature of Moscow broadcasting is the regular relaying of ballets and operas from the Bolshoi Theatre, or Grand Opera House, Theatre Square. As the home of the famous Imperial Russian Ballet, Moscow has always been a prominent artistic centre, and the performances at the Grand Opera House and the other theatres are of the highest standard.

The little dancing lights began to flicker in the black eyes.

"I see that I will have to put it into words of one syllable so you will understand," she began sweetly. "In Maryland and Virginia, Mr. Hatfield, there are always many guests coming and going and three or four more never make any difference. I am not familiar enough with life in Arizona to—"

"O.K., O.K.," he growled. "Forget it. Let it slide. Shut up and give your ears a chance."

"And you don't have to be insulting—"

"I'm sorry, Lady Patrick. On bended knees, wallowing in self-abasement—"

"Oh, you shut up!"

The elevator opened and he lined out ahead of her, his floppy hat crushed down over his forehead, his heels smacking the tiles.

Lil read the telegram hurriedly.

I AM GOING TO BE MURDERED STOP I CAN'T GO TO THE POLICE STOP SET YOUR OWN FREE AND HELP ME STOP SIT IN END SEAT MIDDLE AISLE SEVENTH ROW CRITERION THEATRE FIRST SHOW TODAY IF WILLING STOP FURTHER DETAILS WILL BE SUPPLIED.

"Back to the office and find out all you can about this, Jimmy," Pat ordered the messenger. "Where it was filed, how filed, who filed it, and anything else you can get. I want to know all about it."

He was flat on his back, bound hand and foot, on the floor of the cabin of the launch.

The blow on the head that had knocked him out had cut his scalp and his face was smeared with blood.

The gun barrel, pointed downward at him, wavered. Then very slowly it was lowered.

"Last chance!" Tolmie's voice was thick and shaky. "Will you throw in with us?"

He slithered toward me. My own knife was out and I gripped it in front of me and waited. Now my great-bodied adversary advanced inch by inch. He circled like a boxer seeking an opening. He bent sideways, crouched, then suddenly straightened in a lunge. To lessen, the impact of his drive, I heaved desperately against the wall of water at my back, dislodging it with scarce an inch to spare, for divers move underwater like figures in slow motion pictures.

Power on another occasion was entering a cafe and accidentally jostled a lady who was being escorted by a young dandy. The cavalier (he was the lady's son) insisted on calling out the famous duellist for the supposed insult. Power good-humouredly sought to explain, but the hot-headed gallant wouldn't listen, and insisted so much upon fighting that the elder man at last consented. The lady (knowing Power's reputation as a duellist) drew him aside.

"And do you think this attack will come soon?"

"Not later than tonight," asserted Liston. "Perhaps sooner. That message from the plane, the call for mass meetings and all will force Foresti into action."

Then the telephone which stood on the table between them rang. The publisher had given orders that the phone was to ring for but one reason. He snatched the instrument and listened.

"Yeah. You're right." Butcher stood up. "Let's carry him to one of the tents, get him out of the sun. I bet by tomorrow he has a sweet mess of gangrene, or something worse."

"What could be worse?" Picadilly wanted to know as he helped Butcher carry the wounded Vargas to one of the tents.

"I don't know. Pain, I suppose. If he has to linger on and be in pain." He shut his lips together grimly. "But he won't. I'll take care of that."

"Shudderin' thought!"

Pat Holliday guffawed, his voice harsh with biting sarcasm. "Fly a plane in this flood? You're crazy!" He pushed his hands against Hansen's chest. "Get away and leave me alone. I'm clearing out of here, I tell you. I wouldn't fly your mail fifty feet even if the sun was shining and there wasn't a cloud in sight."

All this only seems to prove that pets are all right in their own place, but if we had a place like that we would put some of our blasted relatives there. (B I.1.12–13)

As slippery as it is intriguing, this concoction also suggests the methodical madness of *At Swim*. The ambiguity of the preface's "eleven or twelve" lets us in on the game. We are supposed to be baffled by our "location" at any given time, questioning how we arrived, guessing at our destination. The mathematics employed to determine "cost" proves characteristically deceptive. If even a very bad novel cost a good sevenansixpence, either that twelfth novel was more than twice as expensive as the rest, or we've gotten a bargain on something like thirteen and two-thirds works. The effort to match these numbers with the "pith and cream" excerpts proves just as nugatory; the figures, appropriately, never balance.

The contest here, over modulating verbal scrimmage lines, takes place between scenes; reading from left to right and from top to bottom, we are meant to confuse where one excerpt ends and another begins. Is the "I" of paragraph two the "Solitaire" of the first? And is this "white man" the same person shrieking in paragraph five? Changes of point of view and proper names may indicate switches to new novels but, just as often, ambiguous nouns and pronouns blur the boundaries. Could Solitaire's "difficult position" be the white man's endeavor to "stop this thing?" Might the "one way to do it" be the "chance" which commences as "I leaped upon the stone?" Making one's way from jail, out an elevator, aboard a boat, underwater, into a cafe, toward a tent, off a mail plane, in the place of pets, the reader revels in the anarchic confusion which *At Swim* will pick up and thoroughly promote.

The merit of such controlled chaos is the way it urges the reader to question the procedure through which we usually make sense of novels and everyday life. "Hash" obtrusively and extravagantly flouts the notions of "beginning" and "end" as it resists our urge to construct form based on linear, sequential fabrications. Familiar, paternal narrative structures are exposed as phony—no more valid than the white man's conception of evolution in excerpt two (or is it still one?). *At Swim* will self-consciously subvert these operations more dramatically with a narrative more fractured than "Hash"'s fitful telegram.

By the spring of 1934, O'Brien was ready to call it quits with *Comhthrom Feinne* and focus his "spare-time literary activities" on *Blather,* scheduled to come out that August.[14] After his three-year reign, Brother Barnabas deserved and designed a dramatic send-off for himself. His "final" article, "Scenes in a Novel," displays O'Brien's early fascination with the limitations imposed by and the emancipations enabled by precarious authorial control. The theoretical possibility of language betraying an author will become a focal concern in *At Swim.* Characters such as Furriskey, Lamont, and Shanahan will attempt to determine their own existences, to go their own ways, while an author/offspring such as Orlick Trellis will attempt to write his "father" out of existence by inscribing his death. "Scenes in a Novel" also serves as a postmortem examination of the ways an author might creatively eradicate himself through the act of writing.

SCENES IN A NOVEL
By Brother Barnabas
(Probably Posthumous).

I am penning these lines, dear reader, under conditions of great emotional stress, being engaged, as I am, in the composition of a posthumous article. The great blots of sweat which gather on my brow are instantly decanted into a big red handkerchief, though I know the practice is ruinous to the complexion, having regard to the open pores and the poisonous vegetable dyes that are used nowadays in the Japanese sweat-shops. By the time these lines are in neat rows of print, with no damn overlapping at the edges, the writer will be in Kingdom Come.* (See Gaelic quotation in 8-point footnote.)

I have rented Trotsky's villa in Paris, though there are four defects in the lease (three reckoning by British law) and the drains are—what shall I say?—just a *leetle* bit Gallic. Last week, I set about the melancholy task of selling up my little home. Auction followed auction. Priceless books went for a mere song, and invaluable songs, many of them of my own composition, were ruthlessly exchanged for loads of books. Stomach-pumps and stallions went for next to nothing, while my ingenious home-made typewriter, in perfect order except for two faulty characters, was knocked down for four and tuppence. I was finally stripped of all my possessions, except for a few old articles of clothing upon which I had waggishly placed an enormous reserve price. I was in some doubt about a dappled dressing-gown of red fustian, bordered with a pleasing grey piping. I finally decided to present it to the nation. The Nation, however, acting through one of its accredited Sanitary Inspectors, declined the gift—rather churlishly I thought—and pleading certain statutory prerogatives, caused the thing to be burnt in a yard off Chatham Street within a stone's throw of the house where the Brothers Sheares played their last game of *taiplis*. Think of that! When such things come to pass, as Walt Whitman says, you re-examine philosophies and religions. Suggestions as to compensation were pooh-poohed and sallies were made touching on the compulsory acquisition of slum property. You see? If a great mind is to be rotted or deranged, no meanness or no outrage is too despicable, no maggot or officialdom is too contemptible to perpetrate it . . . . the ash of my dressing-gown, a sickly wheaten colour, and indeed, the whole incident reminded me forcibly of Carruthers McDaid.†

Carruthers McDaid is a man I created one night when I had swallowed nine stouts and felt vaguely blasphemous. I gave him a good

---

*"Truagh sin, a leabhair bhig bháin
Tiocfaidh lá, is ba fíor,
Déarfaidh neach os cionn do chláir
Ní mhaireann an lámh do scríobh."
†Who is Carruthers McDaid, you ask?

but worn out mother and an industrious father, and coolly negativing fifty years of eugenics, made him a worthless scoundrel, a betrayer of women and a secret drinker. He had a sickly wheaten head, the watery blue eyes of the weakling. For if the truth must be told, I had started to compose a novel and McDaid was the kernel or the fulcrum of it. Some writers have started with a good and noble hero and traced his weakening, his degradation and his eventual downfall; others have introduced a degenerate villain to be enobled and uplifted to the tune of twenty-two chapters, usually at the hands of a woman—"She was not beautiful, but a shortened nose, a slightly crooked mouth and eyes that seemed brimful of a simple complexity seemed to spell a curious attraction, an inexplicable charm." In my own case, McDaid, starting off as a rank waster and a rotter, was meant to sink slowly to absolutely the last extremities of human degradation. Nothing, absolutely nothing, was to be too low for him, the wheaten-headed hound. . . .

I shall never forget the Thursday when the thing happened. I retired to my room at about six o'clock, fortified with a pony of porter and two threepenny cigars, and manfully addressed myself to the achievement of Chapter Five. McDaid, who for a whole week had been living precariously by selling kittens to foolish old ladies and who could be said to be existing on the immoral earnings of his cat, was required to rob a poor-box in a church. But no! Plot or no plot, it was not to be.

"Sorry, old chap," he said, "but I absolutely can't do it."

"What's this, Mac," said I, "getting squeamish in your old age?"

"Not squeamish exactly," he replied, "but I bar poor-boxes. Dammit, you can't call me squeamish. Think of that bedroom business in Chapter Two, you old dog."

"Not another word," said I sternly, "you remember that new shaving brush you bought?"

"Yes."

"Very well. You burst the poor-box or it's anthrax in two days."

"But, I say, old chap, that's a bit thick."

"You think so? Well, I'm old fashioned enough to believe that your opinions don't matter."

We left it at that. Each of us firm, outwardly polite, perhaps, but determined not to yield one tittle of our inalienable rights. It was only afterwards that the whole thing came out. Knowing that he was a dyed-in-the-wool atheist, I had sent him to a revivalist prayer meeting, purely for the purpose of scoffing and showing the reader the blackness of his soul. It appears that he remained to pray. Two days afterwards, I caught him sneaking out to Gardiner Street at seven in the morning. Furthermore, a contribution to the funds of a well known charity, a matter of four-and-sixpence in the name of Miles Caritatis was not, I understand, unconnected with our proselyte. A character ratting on his creator and exchanging the pre-destined hangman's rope for a halo is something new. It is, however, only one factor in my impending dissolution. Shaun Svoolish, my hero, the composition of whose heroics have cost me many a sleepless day, has formed an alliance with a slavey in Griffith Avenue; and Shiela, his "steady," an exquisite creature I produced for the sole purpose of loving him and becoming his wife, is apparently to be given the air. You see? My carefully thought-out plot is turned inside out and goodness knows where this individualist flummery is going to end. Imagine sitting down to finish a chapter and running bang into an unexplained slavey at the turn of a page! I reproached Shaun, of course.

"Frankly, Shaun," I said, "I don't like it."

"I'm sorry," he said. "My brains, my brawn, my hands, my body are willing to work for you, but the heart! Who shall say yea or nay to the timeless passions of a man's heart? Have you ever been in love? Have you ever—?"

"What about Shiela, you shameless rotter? I gave her dimples, blue eyes, blond hair and a beautiful soul. The last time she met you, I rigged her out in a blue swagger outfit, brand new. You now throw the whole lot back in my face. . . . Call it cricket if you like, Shaun, but don't expect me to agree."

"I may be a prig," he replied, "but I know what I like. Why can't I marry Bridie and have a shot at the Civil Service?"

"Railway accidents are fortunately rare," I said finally, "but when they happen they are horrible. Think it over."

"You wouldn't dare!"

"O, wouldn't I? Maybe you'd like a new shaving brush as well."

And that was that.

Treason is equally widespread among the minor characters. I have been confronted with a Burmese shanachy, two corner boys, a barmaid and five bus drivers, none of whom could give a satisfactory explanation of their existence or a plausible account of their movements. They are evidently "friends" of my characters. The only character to yield me undivided and steadfast allegiance is a drunken hedonist who is destined to be killed with kindness in Chapter Twelve. *And he knows it!* Not that he is any way lacking in cheek, of course. He started nagging me one evening.

"I say, about the dust jacket—"

"Yes?"

"No damn vulgarity, mind. Something subtle, refined. If the thing was garish or cheap, I'd die of shame."

"Felix," I snapped, "mind your own business."

Just one long round of annoyance and petty persecution. What is troubling me just at the moment, however, is a paper-knife. I introduced it in an early scene to give Father Hennessy something to fiddle with on a parochial call. It is now in the hands of McDaid. It has a dull steel blade, and there is evidently something going on. The book is seething with conspiracy and there have been at least two whispered consultations between all the characters, including two who have not yet been officially created. Posterity taking a hand in the destiny of its ancestors, if you know what I mean. It is too bad. The only objector, I understand, has been Captain Fowler, the drunken hedonist, who insists that there shall be no foul play until Chapter Twelve has been completed; and he has been over-ruled.

Candidly, reader, I fear my number's up.

* *

I sit at my window thinking, remembering, dreaming. Soon I go to my room to write. A cool breeze has sprung up from the west, a clean wind that plays on men at work, on boys at play and on women who seek to police the corridors, live in Stephen's Green and feel the heat of buckshee turf. . . .

It is a strange world, but beautiful. How hard it is, the hour of parting. I cannot call the Guards, for we authors have our foolish pride. The destiny of Brother Barnabas is sealed, sealed for aye.

I must write!

These, dear reader, are my last words. Keep them and cherish them. Never again can you read my deathless prose, for my day that has been a good day is past.

Remember me and pray for me.

Adieu! (*CF* VIII.2.29–30)[15]

"Scenes in a Novel" is arguably O'Brien's most vital and suggestive piece of writing prior to *At Swim*. As early as 1934, he is clearly trying out numerous elements which figure prominently in his first novel. His attraction to such experimental stylistic flummery and theoretical foul play provides the impetus behind the exorbitant fiction published in 1939.

In many ways, the Brother Barnabas of this article anticipates the college student constructed to narrate *At Swim*. The "few old articles of clothing" that the Brother saves from the auction look like hand-me-downs from Stephen Dedalus. Although the cleric loses his red fustian dressing gown, most of his wardrobe will be bequeathed to *At Swim*'s anonymous narrator so that he might participate in the tradition of the unhygenic, verminous, Dublin undergraduate. Like Joyce's Stephen, *At Swim*'s aspiring author turns up a likely catalyst for his scratching: "A growing irritation in various parts of my body led me to examine my bedclothes and the discovery of lice in large numbers was the result of my researches" (*AS* 60).

The Brother also shares with *At Swim*'s student narrator a self-conscious urge to repudiate traditional narrative patterns. Instead of a noble character experiencing a tragic fall, or a cad being redeemed by the feminine mystique, Carruthers McDaid, like John Furriskey, is designed to begin at the bottom and then run downhill. The rigidity of conventional structures is also satirized by comically literalizing clichés. Captain Fowler, the drunken hedonist, a.k.a. Felix, is destined to be "killed with kindness" in chapter twelve, but he hints that he might prematurely "die of shame" if the dustjacket is not suitably decorous.

Character traits and types which appear in *At Swim* are also being worked out here. Shaun Svoolish's Shiela, with "dimples, blue eyes, blond hair and a beautiful soul" serves as a model for Sheila Lamont, "a very beautiful and refined girl" (*AS* 86). Both are characters of purpose (as are all of Dermot Trellis's). Shaun's Shiela is created "for the sole purpose of loving him and becoming his wife" while Sheila Lamont is produced "in order to show how an evil man can debase the highest and lowest in the same story" (*AS* 86). Carruthers McDaid not only sets a pattern for John Furriskey's "narrative development" but, even more importantly, both are "born" through the most curious labor. "Coolly negativing fifty years of eugenics," the Brother creates McDaid fully formed and apparently quite capable of taking care of himself. This technique is worked out in *At Swim* as the theory of "aestho-autogamy":

> There was nothing unusual in the appearance of Mr. John Furriskey but actually he had one distinction that is rarely encountered—he was born at the age of twenty-five and entered the world with a memory but without a personal experience to account for it. His teeth were well formed but stained by tobacco, with two molars filled and a cavity threatened in the left canine. His knowledge of physics was moderate and extended to Boyle's Law and the Parallelogram of Forces. (*AS* 9–10)

The paper knife which McDaid filches also alludes to the problematics of presence. Created on and of paper, it nevertheless acquires a steel blade through the alchemy of words. A priest requires bread and wine to pull off his magic act, but the Brother's transubstantiation involves cheaper articles—ink and paper. Anticipating the rebellion against the author Trellis in *At Swim*, the Brother fears that his "self" is directly endangered by the literary "presence" of McDaid and the knife.

The explanation of the object's purpose is just as comically suggestive. Apparently, Father Hennessy needs "something to fiddle with on a parochial call." The adjective "parochial" empowers one of O'Brien's uncharacteristically subtle puns. Since the w.c. is colloquially referred to, at least by *At Swim*'s Orlick, as "the parochial house, the bathroom, you know," Father Hennessy's call might be more than natural (*AS* 259). If he needs a substitute plaything to "fiddle" with on such a visit, we suspect that he hasn't outgrown the misdemeanor Stephen Dedalus made famous. Like the student narrator of *At Swim*, he is probably prone to "opening his granny," breaking the law in his own hands.

Such interpretation may be eccentric, but the fun of the text is the way it suggests without confirming such possibilities. And the structure of the article, springing from wild associations of ideas, encourages unconventional speculations. After all, Carruthers McDaid only emerges because the Brother's typewriter has "two faulty characters," and the "sickly wheaten colour" of the burnt robe coincidentally reminds the author of the "sickly wheaten" tint of "the rotter"'s hair.

The most significant correspondence between this article and *At Swim*, however, is the complicated, comedic character rebellion: "Posterity taking a hand in the destiny of its ancestors, if you know what I mean." Here, as in *At Swim*, O'Brien explores the extent to which an author's progeny—words or constructs made with words—might assume and exercise, at least temporarily, a presence and authority of their own. The mutiny of characters serves as more than an interesting plot device; it is a metaphoric challenge to the supposed "inalienable rights" of an author. O'Brien presents a writer's authority in and over a text as highly problematic; it is volatile, precarious, up-for-grabs with every stroke of the pen. McDaid enjoys an existence beyond that ascribed: he sells kittens to support himself between gigs for the Brother and exerts his will independent of his author, conspiring to Oedipally do in dad. Yet the Brother can still transform a shaving brush into anthrax or add a devastating railroad accident to preserve his safety. In *At Swim*, Trellis's characters find themselves free to go about their own business while their author sleeps. They augment their independence by drugging Trellis's porter so that he sleeps twenty out of twenty-four hours. With their "free" time, some open up a sweet shop, others hold tea parties, and an enterprising bunch attempts to write their own novel in which they liquidate their author.

In both the article and the novel, however, this intriguing contest for authority is left up in the air with O'Brien deftly avoiding taking sides. Although the Brother fears that his "number's up," he paradoxically affirms, *"I must write."* And Trellis is accidentally spared elimination when the pages of his manuscript, which authorize the existence of the rebellious characters, are unwittingly burnt by a maid. The absence of a firm resolution—the heightening of instability—urges our careful consideration of language as a seditious commodity, ever-ready to buck intention.

At times, O'Brien may appear as merely a clever fellow largely interested in self-congratulatory word games. To be sure, he is a showoff, but I believe the show is telling. Many of his university publications present witty, humorous, and thoughtful probings of the vital theoretical interactions negotiated between an author and modes of discourse. His exploration of textual and technical problematics is the attempt to locate covert, complex constraints within the language—those linguistic elements and procedures which can disqualify a writer's authority. These procedures—coercive to the extent that they go unchallenged—range from conventional narrative networks to the notion that words easily and simply refer to things.

As a literary counterpuncher, O'Brien displays his skills best in response to formidable opposition. Whether he calls himself B. UaN., Brother Barnabas, Count O'Blather, Flann O'Brien, or Myles na Gopaleen, this writer intentionally seeks out and actively resists discursive strategies which threaten to swallow his subjectivity. His literary play is an invigorating exercise of power, for it tenaciously, if temporarily, affirms a willful self and a pleasure in presence.

2

At Swim-Two-Birds: Exorbitance and the Early Manuscripts

Materiem superabat opus.

—Ovid

In the most comprehensive study to date, *Flann O'Brien: A Critical Introduction to His Writings*, Anne Clissmann says: "O'Brien had a command of at least three languages (and probably more). The awareness of linguistic nuance that resulted from this command reveals itself in the style of all his novels and in the 'Cruiskeen Lawn' column. I am aware of this but incapable of examining the characteristics of his style."[1] Surprisingly, Clissmann and most other critics shy away from the questions of style and the semantic tensions which enable and animate *At Swim-Two-Birds*. O'Brien's awareness of "linguistic nuance" enables the vital wordplay of the novel and, simultaneously, leads him to suspect that what might be termed a "command" of language is—at best and for anyone—desperately precarious. An examination of the revisions in the early, unpublished manuscripts of *At Swim* reveals O'Brien actively engaged in exploring how words might operate, and delightfully involved in negotiating with the problematics of various fields of arrangement.[2]

I. A. Richards, speaking of a "very strange phenomenon constantly appearing in the arts," observes: "what is most essential often seems to be done as it were inadvertently, to be a byproduct, an accidental concomitant."[3] By some such seeming or designed inadvertence, O'Brien is essentially "re-imagining" the novel and confronting, under the guise of mere fun, the serious ramifications of writing. *At Swim* smuggles in the basic and, for me, most interesting questions: What does it mean to "author"? Can the stability of a text be trusted? What is the career of a word on a page in its interactions with other words?

Of course these questions are not unique to O'Brien and cannot finally be resolved. Nonetheless, O'Brien's fascination with the properties of language is, in many respects, the center of his concern as a novelist. The complications and excitement of *At Swim* issue from the way writing is approached from different directions through a medley of voices. Getting there had better be more than half the fun because we never really arrive. As the not-so-Good-Fairy declares: "Answers do not matter so much as questions. . . . A good question is very hard to answer. The better the question the harder the answer. There is no answer at all to a good question" (*AS* 291).

The task of *placing* characters will be discussed later; for now, we need not concern ourselves with conventional problems of identity. John Furriskey (whose presence depends on the authenticity of "aestho-autogamy") stumbles into the twilight zone of the novel when he states: "The voice was first. . . . The human voice. The voice was Number One. Anything that came after was only an imitation of the voice" (*AS* 215). I intend to show that O'Brien questions the naive confidence of such a statement. He tries to get in back of the human voice and test the possibility that something precedes "Number One." On a number line, zero and irrational integers might obviate the Pooka Fergus MacPhellimey's assurance that "truth is an odd number" and Number One is "the Prime Truth" (*AS* 155). In discourse, latent procedures of arrangement might shape possible thoughts and statements, complicating speaking and writing. If to *author* is to test writing as a projection of self, as I think it is in *At Swim*, O'Brien explores whether and to what extent a voice can achieve presence through a style.

One of the most obvious and successful means of prompting our reconsideration of language is the disruption of arrangements we are used to perceiving in life, in the novel, and through the constructs of criticism. Reading *At Swim*, our position is somewhat like that of the student narrator watching a game of pool: "The craft of billiards was unfamiliar to me but in politeness I watched the quick darting of the balls, endeavouring to deduce from the results of a stroke the intentions which preceded it" (*AS* 70–71). The narrator's effort to think back through a shot is founded on conscious operations which, if applied to the reading of *At Swim*, leave the audience "snookered." The following passage from Hume's *A Treatise of Human Nature* analyzes the fundamental methods of knowing which are ruptured in O'Brien's text:

Here is a billiard-ball lying on the table, and another ball moving towards it with rapidity. They strike; and the ball, which was formerly at rest, now acquires a motion. This is as perfect an instance of the relation of cause and effect which we know either by sensation or reflection. Let us therefore examine it. 'Tis evident that the two balls touched one another before the motion was communicated, and that there was no interval between the shock and the motion. *Contiguity* in time and place is therefore a requisite circumstance to the operation of all causes. 'Tis evident likewise, that the motion, which was the cause, is prior to the motion, which was the effect. *Priority* in time is therefore another requisite circumstance in every cause.[4]

While the narrator's confusion watching billiards stems from his unfamiliarity with procedures and jargon of the game such as "kiss," "massé," and "English," our quandary reading the novel resides in our overfamiliarity with processes and circumstances such as cause and effect, contiguity, and priority. O'Brien himself once said of his text, "it is harder on the head than the worst whiskey."[5] Just as it is only possible to measure the wildness of inebriation against a standard statelike sobriety, it is only possible to measure the exorbitance of *At Swim* against the familiar operations it suspends.

Traditionally, the novel has been considered a "realistic" medium, a genre with direct reference to the world we daily inhabit. The classic novel, especially in the nineteenth century, presents an alternative environment which resembles, represents, and temporarily rivals the environment in which we spend most of our time. Distinguishing some of the "classic offices of the novel," Richard Chase emphasizes "verisimilitude, development, continuity."[6] In the twentieth century, we are so used to reading novelistically (whether thinking about history, listening to the news, or viewing film) that we gloss over the ways our notion of verisimilitude has become a product of development and continuity.

Interestingly, art mirrors reality not so much because specific novelistic events resemble experiences of our everyday world, but because we put together fictional experiences using the same procedures with which we imbue our lives with shape. Our perceptions of time—our methods of measuring duration—fundamentally inform the means by which we establish relationships. In the novel, as well as in life, the primary processes of ordering are perceived as linear, sequential, developmental, and causal. In *Time and the Novel*, Patricia Tobin explains:

it is not the singular event, but the seriality of events about which we hold hard and fast conceptions. The realistic novel convinces us, not because the contents of the fictional world resemble our own, but because it structures experience in the same way we do; what is essential to the illusion of reality is not what happens but how it happens.[7]

In *Beginnings*, Edward Said observes that novelistic characters and societies are believable because they "mirror a process of engenderment or beginning and growth possible and permissible for the mind to imagine."[8] The progress of a character and the development of a novel are easily imagined because the process of establishing structure resembles the genealogical procedure of the family. Like a parent begetting a child, one event preceding another is invested with the authority of priority. To come before in time entails the privilege of chronological succession, the power to inaugurate. Denis Donoghue explains: "If one thing happens after another, we assume that it has happened because of the other. In reading a novel, we assume that the events of the fifth chapter depend on the events in the preceding four."[9] The arrangements described here pertain to the methods of making and reading sentences as well as to the larger parts of the novel. An "event" may be a word in a sentence as well as a scene in a chapter. In this sense, Michel Foucault reminds us that time dictates "the linear model of speech (and partly at least of writing), in which all events succeed one another, without any effect of coincidence and superposition."[10]

Against such a time-honored tradition, *At Swim* presents itself as a revisionist text which repeatedly begins a development and just as repeatedly puts off its completion or closure to another time that may or may not occur in the novel. O'Brien goes out of his way to transgress the boundaries usually thought to delineate the territory of the novel. He challenges the conventional systems of coherence dominated by temporality as he accentuates discontinuity and distorts textual superimpositions made possible through memory. Like his character Shanahan inserting his tobacco-stained finger in the texture of Orlick's story, O'Brien repeatedly causes "a lacuna in the palimpsest" (268). And like Laurence Sterne, he comically rebukes "a vicious taste which has crept into thousands . . . of reading straight forwards."[11]

In his Preface to *The American*, Henry James presents a definition of "romance" which fits some of the experimentation of *At Swim*. James states that romance often focuses on liberated experience:

experience, disengaged, disembroiled, disencumbered, exempt from
the conditions that we usually know and attach to it and, if we wish so
to put the matter, drag upon it, and operating in a medium which
relieves it, in a particular interest, of the inconvenience of a related, a
measurable state, a state subject to all our vulgar communities.[12]

I particularly like James's way of defining by telling us what
something is not. His repetition of the prefix "dis-" and use of the
phrases "exempt from," "relieves it . . . of" attempt to arrive at a
type of fiction by obviating certain possibilities. O'Brien frequently employs this strategy. He prompts us to think about less
obvious ways that language operates, especially how absence
determines presence. I will be examining particular instances of
this practice a bit later but, generally speaking, because *At Swim*
excludes the traditional procedures of the novel, it necessarily
refers to them. O'Brien's structures strike us as exciting and worth
scrutiny to the extent that they are different from our expectations.

James also points out that experience offered by romance—and,
I would propose, by this strange novel—is liberated and liberating
to the degree that its medium is freed from the usual concepts of
measurable relationship. In *At Swim*, this means disencumbering
discourse from the "drag" of sequential, causal ordering.
O'Brien's particular interest in seeking such exemptions is to
involve us in verbal expressions on his terms. He illustrates that
outside the conventional schema of novels, the "spare-time literary activity" of inscribing is less stable than it is within them, but
that the opportunities for exciting linguistic play are well worth
the risks.

Despite my appropriation of James's definition, *At Swim* is no
more a "romance" than it is an "anti-novel." O'Brien's she-
nanigans never cancel novelistic norms. Rather they self-consciously deviate from well-worn paths. With the understanding
that any critical label is, at best, a convenient approximation, I
prefer to think of *At Swim* as O'Brien's most "exorbitant novel."

"Exorbitance" may be defined as "a divergence or aberration
from the prescribed or ordinary track; eccentricity" (OED). Exorbitance also conveys a deliberate excessiveness, extravagance. An
interesting aspect of exorbitance presents itself when we think in
terms of celestial bodies revolving around one another in space.
The orbit of a planet around a sun, or a moon around a planet, is
relatively "fixed" by the gravitational pull of the larger mass,
which tempers the satellite's inertial urge to shoot off in a straight

line. Although no circuit is perfectly round and all deviate slightly, "orbit" implies a relatively stable working relationship between gravitational attraction and centrifugal inertia. For a celestial body to go out of its expected orbit, this working relationship must in some way be altered.

When watchers of the skies notice "ex-orbitance," they begin an excited search of the heavens, thrilled by the prospect of explaining errant behavior. Astronomical experience has taught us that planetary perturbation—a variation in the usual orbit—may be the result of an unexpected force attracting the satellite from an eccentric direction, augmenting its inertial urge. The attempt to account for such a force has often led to the discovery of a new presence and radical alterations in our understanding. Thus the existence of an eighth planet in our solar system was posited in 1845, a year before it could be verified telescopically. John Couch Adams and Jean-Joseph Verrier, intrigued by the irregularities in the motion of Uranus, postulated the existence of another planet beyond what was then considered our complete solar system. With the aid of mathematical calculations, Neptune swam into our ken, transforming—by enlarging—our known environment.[13]

Like most planets, the traditional novel usually traverses a predictable path, repeats a familiar shape dictated by the drag of chronological, sequential, causal ordering. The pull of temporality induces conventional fiction to revolve around character and the development of character in time through plot. In "Notes on the Novel," José Ortega y Gasset describes such a dependable orbit when he advises:

> The great novelist, contemptuous of the surface features of his personages, dives down into their soul and returns, clutching in his hand the deep-sea pearl. . . . The material proper of the novel is imaginary psychology. . . . The novel must now revolve about the superior interest emanating from the inner mechanism of the personages. Not in the invention of plots but in the invention of interesting characters lies the best hope of the novel.[14]

According to this recommendation, the exorbitance of *At Swim* dramatizes itself in "improper" material: verbal excess and a fondness for stylistic extravagance. From beginning through all rebeginnings, the reader delights in the infectious thrill of self-conscious negotiations with the materiality of language. O'Brien's text resists the prescriptions of Ortega y Gasset; it never centers on character or on the relationships between characters that constitute a social network. The eccentric pull of an exciting investigation of its own means precludes such a conventional orbit. The novel's subject cannot be man, since it openly suggests that man might very well be a vulnerable construct of language. Rather its subject is discourse itself, varieties of style, and the way any style shapes, distorts, permits, and obviates possible thoughts and statements.

It still remains to substantiate specificially these generalizations; let us look at the text, beginning appropriately with one of the endings. In the "Conclusion of the Book, penultimate," Dermot Trellis, "rated occupier of the Red Swan Hotel" and author of an edifying novel "on sin and the wages attaching thereto," is rescued from the imaginative, gruesome tortures inflicted by his insurgent characters. Dissatisfied with the platitudinous roles assigned to them, Trellis's characters have mutinied and are presently writing their own novel which details the protracted and timely death of their author.

Knocking at Trellis's door to take away a tray, Teresa, a chamber maid at the Red Swan, discovers the room empty. Assuming that the occupant has temporarily gone to "a certain place," Teresa decides to tidy up and revive the fire. In the process, she accidentally saves the master from the plotting of his characters through—what turns out to be—an act of textual deconstruction. Near an open window, Teresa collects some loose paper from the floor and unwittingly kindles the pages of Trellis's manuscript which authorize the existence of the mutinous Furriskey, Shanahan, and Lamont. As the text begins to blaze, the obstreperous characters turned authors are eradicated, transformed into carbon fumes flying up the flue.

Trellis then appears downstairs, knocking at the halldoor in his nightshirt. Very much the worse for wear, complaining of "too much thinking and writing," he voices the muddle of the reader. Seeking bed and rest from such literary chaos, Trellis finds his attention diverted as ours has been:

> He reached unsteadily for the lamp and motioned that she [Teresa] should go before him up the stairs. The edge of her stays, lifting her skirt in a little ridge behind her, dipped softly from side to side with the rise and fall of her haunches as she trod the stairs. It is the function of such garment to improve the figure, to conserve corporal discursiveness, to create the illusion of a finely modulated body. If it betray its own presence when fulfilling this task, its purpose must largely fail.

Ars est celare artem, muttered Trellis, doubtful as to whether he had made a pun. (*AS* 313–14)

The preceding passage offers an apt metaphor for understanding the semimethodical madness of O'Brien's novel. Like Teresa's conspicuous corset, *At Swim* calls attention to itself, flaunting its artificiality. Just as Trellis's eyes follow the motion of Teresa's stays, O'Brien directs the reader's attention to the movement of the novel's machinery. Rather than conceal its art, *At Swim* amplifies the clanking of its ropes, pulleys, and scaffolding. Ortega Y Gasset prescribes that "a novel, in contrast to other literary works, must, while it is read, not be conceived as a novel."[15] O'Brien disagrees, presenting the novel as if it were a play, fulfilling his narrator's assertion that "a satisfactory novel should be a self-evident sham to which the reader could regulate at will the degree of his credulity" (*AS* 33).

Ever since 1939, when reviewers or critics confront *At Swim*, they usually rush into a summary of the plot, evincing a need to stabilize the text within the confines of the more stable orbit previously discussed. The enterprise is often undertaken reluctantly, however, because most good readers sense some vague deficiencies in trying to locate the "several planes and dimensions" of the novel in a synopsis of who authored whom.[16] The critic John Wain reveals a great deal when he reconsiders one of his previous appraisals: "In an essay published in 1962, I made a passing reference to *At Swim-Two-Birds* as a 'Gargantuan comic novel which makes a simultaneous exploration, on four or five levels, of Irish civilization.' The vagueness of 'four or five' suggests that I wasn't counting the levels very carefully or distinguishing them with much clarity."[17]

The imprecision of Wain's numerical assessment indicates something other than a casual carelessness; his equivocation directly issues from the problematic instability of O'Brien's novel. A useful approximation of the form of *At Swim* is the structure imagined by Philip Quarles in *Point Counter Point*:

Put a novelist into the novel. He justifies aesthetic generalizations, which may be intersting—at least to me. He also justifies experiment. Specimens of his work may illustrate other possible or impossible ways of telling a story. And if you have him telling parts of the same story as you are, you can make a variation on the theme. But why draw the line at one novelist inside your novel? Why not a second inside his? And a third inside the novel of the second? And so on to infinity, like those advertisements of Quaker Oats where there's a

Quaker holding a box of oats, on which is a picture of another Quaker holding another box of oats, on which etc., etc. At about the tenth remove, you might have a novelist telling your story in algebraic symbols or in terms of variations in blood pressure, pulse, secretion of ductless glands, and reaction time.[18]

O'Brien shares Quarles's fascination for experimenting with possible ways of telling a story; both wonder about *exorbitant* means of communication and demonstrate a willingness to consider "signs" as procedures. Furriskey's explanation of "how to read a gas meter," for instance, depends on signifiers beyond words—clocklike dials drawn in the dirt—and grounds itself in a mathematical system based on decimal relationships. (If the dials were really clocklike, he would have to work in base twelve.) Similarly, the successful appeal of V. Wright's horseracing advice depends on the punter's subtle movement from a vocabulary of scientific precision into the confidential idiom of sportsmen. "V. Wright, Turf Correspondent" enlists clients as he verbally transforms himself into "Verney" (*AS* 14–15).

Most interesting, however, is the way O'Brien's novel deviates from Quarles's Quaker Oats metaphor. *At Swim* is never a stable "novel-within-a-novel-within-a-novel-within-a-novel"; the image of a Chinese box structure falsely tames the wildness of the text. If O'Brien were to work with the cereal advertisement, he would have a third or fourth generation Quaker break out of the meta-framework, slap the hat off the man who held his image, or begin by consuming the box which enabled his existence.

The novel is neither neatly layered nor hierarchically consistent. The difficulty we have distinguishing characters is due to the players' willful discursiveness. Consider the effort to locate Finn MacCool. From the beginning, we assume that Finn, Furriskey, and The Pooka exist adjacent to one another, as characters of the student narrator, one step below their author. Not until the fifth biographical reminiscence do we find that Finn has been "demoted" a level, serving as a character of Dermot Trellis who is himself a character of the undergraduate. Once we think we have it settled, however, our quandary begins anew. Although instructed by Trellis to act as Peggy's father "and chastise her for her transgressions against the moral law," Finn steps out of his "role" to engage in incest with Peggy while the author sleeps. Complications also abound when Trellis creates Sheila Lamont to serve as a moral function in his salutory book. Overcome by her beauty, the author sexually assaults his character, precipitating the birth of

Orlick Trellis who subsequently tries to write his father out of existence.

Structurally, *At Swim* corresponds with Giambattista Piranesi's intriguing staircases as well as the bewildering school house described in Edgar Allan Poe's "William Wilson." A "palace of enchantment," "there was really no end to its windings—to its incomprehensible subdivisions." Because all the rooms were connected by "three or four steps either in ascent or descent," the occupants could never be sure of their location, on which story they stood: "Then the lateral branches were innumerable—inconceivable—and so returning in upon themselves, that our most exact ideas in regard to the whole mansion were not very far different from those with which we ponder upon infinity."[19] The contemplation of infinity is more properly the subject of *The Third Policeman*, but the disorientation described here is carefully cultivated in *At Swim*.

Objecting to Finn's manner of authoring, Lamont complains: "I mean to say . . . whether a yarn is tall or small I like to hear it well told. I like to meet a man who can take in hand to tell a story and not make a balls of it while he's at it. I like to know where I am, do you know. Everything has a beginning and an end" (*AS* 89). Any reader of Lamont's disposition misses most of the fun of *At Swim*. O'Brien deliberately befuddles the reader and frustrates the mind which wants to sort and organize. Any attempt to accommodate the novel to a systematic structure falls short because the text deliberately resists procedural patterns grounded in traditional rules of coherency. Making "a balls of it," emphasizing exorbitant ways of putting together a plot or a sentence, O'Brien encourages us to reconsider the enterprise of making sense through words while we are ourselves being made by words.

At Swim exhibits O'Brien's uneasiness with the idea of an author as the origin or source of a statement, his disillusionment with the naive assurance that naming corresponds with control. The focus on parricide—with characters trying to do in their author—encourages the reflection that, within any of the multiple fragments, anonymous procedures of arrangement may surreptitiously govern. If the novel centers on anything, it is "verbal *performance*" which, according to Michel Foucault, dramatizes the struggle of an inquiring mind to realize hidden "rules of formation" which influence every act of speaking and writing.[20] Of course, O'Brien is playful and parodic where Foucault is disciplined and scientific, but both share a concern for the extent to which all authors are at the mercy of the statements they think they issue. Through the activities of the undergraduate, O'Brien questions how much of his writing is the appropriation and transformation of styles, and how much of it is appropriated and formed by styles.

The early, unpublished manuscripts of *At Swim* (hereafter referred to as *MS1* and *MS2*) exhibit O'Brien investigating the ramifications of writing and testing the volatile, unreliable properties of language. From the very beginning of *MS1*, we are impressed with O'Brien's healthy perception of words as malleable artifacts. The first leaf of the manuscript (unnumbered but headed "Personal") is composed of a number of seemingly random jottings which suggest quite tellingly how O'Brien will treat language in this novel. The autograph notes are scribbled and scrawled haphazardly on an unlined leaf of typing paper. The jottings tend to wander all over the page, refusing to be accommodated to the usual orders or hierarchies imposed by left-to-right, top-to-bottom sequences. Free from traditional patterns of organization, O'Brien tries out ideas and names of characters, often repeating words or portions of words. For instance, the heading *Personal* is partially reinscribed as *Pers*. This might be a fragment of *Personal* or might even be leading to *Person* or *Personnel*, important titles which head a list of characters three pages later. The word "Engles" is jotted twice with the letter *E* repeated twice and the fragment *Eng* once. Similarly, the phrase "a poor bastard" is toyed with four times and variations of the word "Nerves" wander all over the page as *Ner, Nervii*, and *NERVES* outlined in darker pen. Not all of these jottings are decipherable, but important attitudes toward language are prominently suggested. The notes, including the word "Byrne" and various renditions of the letter *A*, indicate O'Brien's tendency to see and use words as corporal material, opaque instruments of invention. Not only does he often fragment these artifacts, he displays a flair for rewriting words in various fonts. He indicates, from the beginning, how he perceives language as textured, as if a different font or type of letter-making alters the way language signifies and means. By altering the style of the inscription, he explores how he might alter the message conveyed.

This view of words as plastic material for making is evident throughout *MS1*, but two revisions are especially worth noting at this time. After Orlick is born, he is showered with gifts by the Pooka, Good Fairy, and the rest of the company. The newborn begins an ornate thank-you speech but then, as if overcome with emotion, runs out of words:

Your kind gesture is one of these fortuitous felicities that banish for a
time at least the inevitable conviction that wells up in the heart of
every newcomer to this world that life is empty and hollow,
disproportionately trivial compared with the trouble and the rigours
of entering it. Gentlemen, with the exception of my mother, you are
the only people I have met. Your interest in my advent is puzzling but
very pleasant to encounter, and I thank you with all my heart. Your
gifts, they are—
    He searched in the air with his red hand for new words. (*MS1* 198)

The last sentence, which was typed in *MS1*, was later emended in
pen to read:

He searched *for a word* with his red hand *as if to pull one from the air*.
(*MS1* 198, *AS* 208 [italics added])

This is the kind of revision that, at first glance, may seem slight,
but I am arguing that it indicates significant priorities. The new
version, incorporated in *MS2* and the novel, highlights the activity of physically extending an arm up and pulling at air. Orlick
reaches up and waves a hand around his immediate person as if
words, like elements composing a child's mobile suspended
above, were capable of being tangibly grasped. Ironically,
O'Brien's newly composed simile, "as if to pull one [a word] from
the air," is never fulfilled by his newly formed character/author.
Orlick's failure to accommodate language to his will comically
underscores the precariousness of his elaborately stylized speech
of thanks.
    Another key revision further emphasizes O'Brien's focus on
text as malleable material. Later in the novel, Orlick interrupts the
rendition of the tortures of Trellis as he excuses himself to use the
w.c. Shanahan, Furriskey, and Lamont take advantage of his
absence to author their own scripts of Trellis's demise. When they
hear Orlick returning, we encounter another purple passage with
telling revisions.
    The typescript of *MS1* reads:

Noises, peripatetic and external, came faintly upon the gathering in
the midst of their literary composition. Lamont acted with coolness,
resource and cunning.

O'Brien improves the passage with these additions:

Noises, peripatetic and external, came faintly upon the gathering in the midst of their *creative* composition *and spare-time literary activity.* Lamont *handled what promised to be an awkward situation* with coolness and cunning. (*MS1* 252, *AS* 263–64 [italics added])

First, the *creativity* of selecting and conglomerating words is highlighted while the supercilious "literariness" is deemphasized, relegated to "spare-time" status. Second, the replacement of the verb "acted" with "handled" proves most significant. Lamont "handled what promised to be awkward situation" by deftly handling words as if they were a magician's disappearing artifacts. The problem these new authors face has been caused by their inventive amendments to Orlick's story. What better way to extricate themselves and to absolve their interference than by amending the amendments, adding more written additions which "erase" their previous efforts? Lamont inscribes a brief passage in which the Pooka magically transports himself and Trellis back to the exact time, place, and position in which Orlick left them a quarter of an hour ago. Lamont *handles* language to effect a curious addition to the text which states that it excises the prior renditions of Shanahan and Furriskey. O'Brien's contradictory addition/eradication is enabled by his sense for treating words, fragments, and even fonts of letters like tactile entities to be creatively manhandled.

Several other notes and revisions in *MS1* display O'Brien testing the waters of authorship, never satisfied with his footing on the grounds of an author's control. The third unnumbered leaf of the manuscript (the second is blank) also offers eclectic phrases and fragments of words which prove pregnant with possibilities. The top left-hand corner of the page presents one word which eventually dominates the leaf: *Controller.* O'Brien toys with this important aspect of authorship a total of ten times on the page, with *Controller* appearing eight times in full while the fragments *Con* and *C* appear once each. These autograph inscriptions of *Controller* surround the author's name written as *Brian Ó Nualláin* twice and as incomplete portions of the letter *B* twice. With *Brian Ó Nualláin* appearing near the top center and *Controller* surrounding the proud inscription of identity, it seems highly probable that the mind employing the fountain pen was pondering notions of a writer's dominion over words. But the idea of mastering language was highly problematic for O'Brien before, during, and after the composition of *At Swim.* At times, as is suggested in these jottings, O'Brien seems to enjoy the feeling of individual authority derived from superior abilities to select and coordinate words to effect an innovative structure. During these moments, he seems to subscribe to the more traditionally accepted view that words can be employed to create a stable environment beyond themselves. Most of the time, however, O'Brien writes as if he readily admits that any such belief in "authority" is itself merely a temporary "con."

The novel recounts Finn's lament at being abused and deformed by words collected in a sea-blue book. He argues against "a crooked and dishonourable story" which misrepresents his dealings with the Churl in the Puce Great-coat (*AS* 23). The story is actually read aloud in *MS1* but is cut and summarized in the novel. But both *MS1* and the novel postulate that words certainly do have power over people: "Small wonder, said Finn, that Finn is without honour in the breast of a sea-blue book, Finn that is twisted and trampled and tortured for the weaving of a storyteller's book-web. Who but a book-poet would dishonour the God-big Finn for the sake of a gap-worded story" (*AS* 24)? The power of words to assert their authority over a character like Finn—as if telling or inscribing were synonymous with making—is also promoted through the authorship of Orlick who writes and effects the torture of Trellis. But the prominent theme of mutiny—characters rebelling against their author as words successfully resist the writer—certainly complicates any assurance of an author's control.

Precisely because any writer's jurisdiction over words and the systems they compose remains in constant tension and flux, O'Brien repeatedly reinvestigates how words and possible combinations of words might signify. Another seemingly innocuous revision between *MS1* and *MS2* evinces a careful reevaluation of how signifiers operate. In the student narrator's first conversation with his uncle, the two argue about the studying (or lack thereof) which proceeds in the nephew's bedroom. When the uncle questions the amount of studying accomplished behind closed doors, the ostensible protagonist originally responds:

> I made a reply indeterminate and perfunctory, and retired in good order to my bedroom. I had a letter in my pocket and was anxious to read it and light my cigarette. (*MS1* 3)

This rather bland, unimaginative response has been completely transformed in the final revisions of *MS2:*

> I know the studying you do in your bedroom, said my uncle. Damn
> the studying you do in your bedroom.
> I denied this.
>
> *Nature of denial:* Inarticulate, of gesture.
>
> (MS2 5, AS 12–13)

By the time *At Swim* was ready for the printer, this reply was
stressed as a major narrative interruption that underscored the
fragmentation and discontinuity of the novel. O'Brien took great
pains getting the typesetter to accentuate the extra spacing and
italic font dramatizing the interruption. But, more importantly,
the reply became the volatile, undefined signifier which we, the
readers, must give shape to through the active engagement of our
imaginations. The phrase "of gesture" was added in autograph to
MS2 to highlight just how precarious and arbitrary such a denial
might be. The wishy-washy verbal reply of *MS1*, "indeterminate
and perfunctory," now becomes a highly charged physical gesture transforming silence. Each reader can imagine several facial,
hand, or body movements which might suffice as an appropriate
denial, but no reader is ever sure that her imagined denial is *the*
inaudible motion to which the narrator alludes. Any reader who
begins to question the elusive quality of words and networks of
words will certainly enjoy the dialogue O'Brien is fostering with
his audience.

A similar colloquy between O'Brien and his readers is conspic-
ously added to *MS2*. At one point, the narrator and Brinsley are
interrupted in the bedroom by the uncle who proceeds to ha-
rangue both on the best methods for avoiding flu and the rewards
of a religious vocation. As soon as the uncle retires (for a second
time) we confront another intriguing confluence of signifiers:

> In a moment he was gone, this time without return. Brinsley, a
> shadow by the window, performed perfunctorily the movements of a
> mime, making at the same time a pious ejaculation.
>
> *Nature of mime and ejaculation:* Removal of sweat from brow; holy God.
> (*MS2* 33, *AS* 40)

The context, with the two friends desperately wishing the uncle
to leave, provides a recognizable field for such a reaction. The
response, however, begins mysteriously, slowly takes shape, yet
remains malleable and suggestively interpretive. At first, we are
teased with the unspecified gesture and ejaculation. Then these

ambiguous signs begin to acquire shapes with the additional explanation of their "Nature." But, curiously enough, the indirect approach to determining meaning still leaves the reader the task of imagining just how the "removal of sweat" might be acted out and in what tones one might utter the anything-but-pious cliché. Does one wipe away sweat with the back of the hand? With the entire forearm? Wringing the fingers for effect? What would be the appropriate duration, inflection, or amplitude for such a "well known" verbal expression of amazement and relief? In adding such a passage, O'Brien stresses the degree to which he wants to keep the stability of words, gestures, and signs in question. The delay, carefully conveyed through the use of white space, before the intrusion of our hypererudite student writer, transforms what could have been a banal action and cliché into a performance of delightful amusement.

Other examples of O'Brien's fascination with inarticulate signs are added in autograph to the typescript of *MS1*. While Orlick attempts to erase the life of his father, Trellis, by writing him out of existence, he is repeatedly interrupted by Furriskey, Lamont, and Shanahan who want to affirm their participation by commenting on details of the narrative. One such interruption elicits the following response from the character-turned-author: "On his smallest finger, Orlick screwed the cap of his waterman fountain-pen, the one with the fourteen-carat nib; when he unscrewed it again there was a black circle about his finger." At a later date, O'Brien adds in pen:

Symbolism of the foregoing: annoyance. (*MSI* 268, *AS* 282)

The play with signification here centers on the hyperbolic disparity between details of the pen's material nature and the bathetic understatement of the gesture's meaning. O'Brien's autograph addition calls attention to this disparity and plays one means of signifying off the other. The student narrator flaunts his self-serving concern with authoring the details of the pen's configuration and the application of the cap to one phalange. O'Brien then undermines such authorial self-consciousness by having the amateur author add the gratuitous explanation of a simple gesture as a manifestation of impatient displeasure.

The energetic play with language testifies to a vital force emerging as O'Brien constructs *At Swim*. Throughout the composition and revisions of *MS1* and *MS2*, O'Brien is actively experimenting with the various ways words and other fields of discourse might constitute meaning. The humor, confusion, and pleasures of *At Swim* derive from his continuous reinvestigation of the ways language precariously signifies. Words, for O'Brien and for the reader, cannot merely refer to a stable "reality" somewhere out there. Words, gestures, and noises refer to and sound *themselves* as much as they indicate any external object or concept. At the same time, words compete with and abuse other words that have been displaced, that surround them on a page, or that exist elsewhere in this and other texts.

The attention to sounds is everywhere apparent; examples range from the vibrations emitted by Byrne's tea cup clinking its saucer to the specific stimulation of the eardrum caused by Sweeny falling from a thorny tree. Further autograph additions to *MS1*, seemingly innocuous or inconsequential, evince this attentiveness to sounds which proves to be a driving force for much of the prose. When the Pooka and Good Fairy depart on their journey to welcome Orlick into the world, the Pooka's unique amble receives detailed care. Originally, the Pooka crashes through the undergrowth, "treading the lichen with a heavy tread and a light one, a club-step and a footstep" (*MS1*, 161). One brief addition, however, aurally clarifies and enlivens the rhythm and accent of his gait. The passage is emended in hand so that the Pooka walks, "treading the lichen with a heavy tread and a light one, *iambic pentameter*, a club-step and a footstep" (*MS1* 161, *AS* 161, [italics added]). We now hear the Pooka's walk (more than we see it) in the unusual context of classical English verse.

Later in the manuscript and novel, O'Brien humorously suggests how sounds might be entirely misleading. During the trial of Trellis, the Good Fairy is requested to take the stand to testify. O'Brien's first rendition of this scene lacked a significant misunderstanding. The passage first read:

> Let the Good Spirit take the stand, boomed the Pooka.
> I've been in the stand all the time, said the voice, the grand stand.
> Where is this man? asked Mr. Justice Lamphall sharply. If he does not appear quickly I will issue a bench warrant.
> This man has no body on him at all, explained the Pooka. Sometimes I carry him in my waistcoat pocket for days and do not know that he is there. (*MS1* A, inserted between 276 and 277)

By the time O'Brien had made his final revisions for publication, the inserted passage included one key difference:

Let the Good Fairy take the stand, boomed the Pooka.

I've been in the stand all the time, said the voice, the grand stand.

Where is this *woman*? asked Mr. Justice Lamphall sharply. If *she* does not appear quickly I will issue a bench warrant.

This man has no body on him at all, explained the Pooka. Sometimes I carry him in my waistcoat pocket for days and do not know that he is there. (*MS1* A, *AS* 291 [italics added]).

The sex-change in the novel not only accentuates the horseplay of the trial (where the "grand stand" would afford the appropriate view), it also suggests just how misleading sounds might be as indicators of presence or definition. The amplitude, pitch, and timbre of spoken language are just as telling as the articulation of vowels, consonants, and accents. O'Brien keeps us on our toes by emphasizing how the meanings of words depend to a great extent on flexible, volatile, modulating sound vibrations.

Arrangements of words, and the absences of other possible words, obviously inform all interpretations of discourse. O'Brien prompts his readers to reconsider methods through which we decode messages when he decides to teach his audience to read Greek. The comically clever response of the student narrator to Brinsley's proposal on horserace betting indicates O'Brien's attraction to the varieties of meanings conveyed through sound:

> The price given here, said Brinsley from the paper, is ten to one and say that's seven to one at a half-a-crown each way that's twenty-one bob. Buy your book and you have sixteen shillings change.
>
> More by accident than by any mastery of the body, I here expressed my doubts on the proposal by the means of a noise.

> *Title of noise, the Greek version:* πορδή. (*AS* 51)

Such a passage transcends the status of scatalogical humor when we begin to wonder how the noise, which we cannot hear, and the Greek transcription, which most of us cannot read, achieve an indirect presence through the craft of arranging decorous words which envelop and partially purify the air.

As he was reconstituting his manuscript, O'Brien definitely decided that he preferred indirect signifiers that call attention to their own properties while they simultaneously engage the readers' imaginations. One passage added in pen on the verso of a leaf of *MS1* was thoughtfully rejected and modified in the composition of *MS2*. In one scene, the student narrator enters the college searching for Brinsley. He sees instead another fellow student,

Kerrigan, who greets him with a curious salutation. In *MS1*, O'Brien had considered a juvenile, punning exchange: "He came forward and sought to be furnished with a suitable definition of a blunderbus. Being unable for the moment to give this, he explained that a blunderbus was a taxi-cab full of pregnant prostitutes" (*MS1* 67v). Dangling modifiers aside, the play on words is decidedly inferior to the invention O'Brien settled on for the final copy: "He came forward quickly when he saw me and enunciated and answered an obscene conundrum. He then looked away and frowned, waiting intently for my laugh" (*AS* 70). The sophomoric quality of undergraduate growing pains remains as Kerrigan cannot wait to repeat what is probably someone else's witticism. But the novel leaves the conundrum an unspecified mystery, shifting our attention to Kerrigan's craving for applause, a need which the narrator is learning to temper in himself.

O'Brien's preoccupation with the possibilities and limitations inherent in and imposed by various styles of discourse often manifests itself in the student narrator's self-conscious reflections about the language he utters and listens to. One prevalent theme is the narrator's delight in participating with, and eventually circumventing, traditions of rhetorical arrangement. He continually interrupts his narrative to congratulate himself on his apparently newfound facility with tropes. When Brinsley offers to buy a round of pints, our narrator informs us:

> I rejoined that if his finances warranted such generosity, I would raise no objection, but that I (for my part) was no Rockefeller, thus utilizing a figure of speech to convey the poverty of my circumstances.

Name of figure of speech: Synecdoche (or Autonomasia). (*MS1* 49, *AS* 63)

Such a passage is rife with interesting possibilities. Although declaring his monetary poverty, the speaker promotes his own rich diction and sense of arrangement. Words such as "rejoined," "warranted," "utilizing," and phrases such as "raise no objection" and "poverty of my circumstances" prove delightfully intriguing because their ornamental or formal features so blatantly conflict with the banal admission of an absence of pence. The arrangement of the words, moreover, proceeding from a simple declarative clause ("I rejoined that") to causality ("if . . . I would") to antithesis ("but") to causality again ("thus . . .") underscores that the medium really does convey more than a simple message. The speaker conveys, in the sense of transmits, his lack of funds but,

more importantly, conveys, in the sense of transports, the reader/
listener to a realm of thought where words impart more than their
usual meanings. Synecdoche or autonomasia (or more properly
antonomasia) as a figure of speech is colloquially used all the time
by people who have not even encountered the word. But when
we begin to carefully reconsider how a part might stand for the
whole, or how a proper name comes to "convey" a general idea,
we enter the true realm of the novel, the realm of energetic verbal
adventures. Synecdoche, autonomasia, or antonomasia try to en-
liven discourse by highlighting new, untapped possibilities in
discourse. And, like all figures of speech, they depend upon a
precarious, constantly changing milieu of "accepted sense" which
can become enervated and dull or which can become invigorated
and vital through inventive creativity.

We can appreciate some of O'Brien's major stylistic preferences
when we examine the student narrator's introduction to the first
synopsis of his plot. He begins by attentively contrasting the
procedures of writing and reading:

> My literary or spare-time compositions, written not infrequently with
> animation and enjoyment, I always found tedious of subsequent per-
> usal. This sense of tedium is so deeply seated in the texture of my
> mind that I can rarely suffer myself to endure the pain of it. One result
> is that many of my shorter works, even those made the subject of
> extremely flattering *encomia* on the part of friends and acquaintances, I
> have never myself read, nor does my indolent memory enable me to
> recall their contents with a satisfactory degree of accuracy. A hasty
> search for syntactical solecism was the most I could perform. (*AS* 83–
> 84)

The passage opens with the narrator detailing his preference for
the activity of authoring which he terms an engaging operation
producing personal energy and pleasure. The last sentence, however, is the most salient because it locates a tried and trusted
avenue of authorial inspiration and delight. (The spacing of *MS1*
indicates that this concluding remark was added as an important
afterthought. The sentence is noticeably squeezed into the white
space between the end of one paragraph and the beginning of
another) (*MS1* 89). In trying to recall the content of previous
compositions, the narrator searches his memory for "syntactical
solecisms" as if he half-consciously remembers that these unique
arrangements were and are the "source" of his vitality as a writer.
"Solecism," itself a word from "off-the-beaten-path," may be un-

derstood as a nonstandard grammatical construction or a linguistic impropriety, mistake, or incongruity. The narrator, like O'Brien, would certainly search for syntactical solecisms, not to correct them as a proofreader would, but to savor their innovative creativity. These linguistic "improprieties," which flout conventional order, form, and content, are the lifeblood of an imagination which desperately desires to trespass beyond the pale of traditional discourses.

The writer here is seen as one who consciously violates the standard constructions; breaches of "acceptable" arrangements are deliberate and no mistake. To unlearn the inherited narrative formats one must begin by making every effort to undermine their procedures. Too many words, phrases, and arrangements arrive burdened with the baggage of previously determined meanings. To squeeze out drops of new meaning, to compose fiction as if it were "novel," requires the concerted effort to make anew by violating previously authorized arrangements and meanings. The final word of the passage, "perform," represents a significant, astute reconsideration between *MS1* and the published novel. In the addition to *MS1*, O'Brien had originally written "endure." "Perform" is a much better choice because making anew, reconstituting some of the old building blocks and recomposing innovative structures, requires that a writer view the activity as a performance engaging discerning, live audiences.

Another clue to O'Brien's sense of language is contained in an autograph addition to *MS1* which was later omitted in the novel. Before journeying to Orlick's nativity, the Pooka and Good Fairy engage in a lengthy, spirited dialogue canvassing a wild collection of esoteric topics. Originally designated "the Devil" and "the Angel," the Pooka and Good Fairy naturally approach almost all subjects from opposing directions. On the verso of one of the manuscript pages of dialogue, O'Brien had jotted down an autograph note which proves highly suggestive:

> Life is a conflict.
> All movement due to
> conflict between good and evil.
> Therefore God without devil is
> absurd. like a backyard
> without a house. (*MS1* 146v)

This note does not designate a moral position so much as it points to an important attitude about language as a system of shifting tensions. As Saussurean linguistics has insisted, words—as signs—are engaged as networks of conflicts. All movement and meanings arrived at through language depend upon the contentions of differences. According to this note, "backyard," (which is partially defined by its difference from "frontyard" or "back fence") depends for its presence on the existence of, and its conflicts with, a structure we have learned to name "house." This theme of opposing forces creating "identity" recurs several times throughout *MS1*. At one point, Trellis raises the issue through a hypothetical dilemma concerning a streetwalker who uses her profits to build a church (*MS1* 18). But O'Brien is even more direct in another rejected passage from *MS1* when he has Trellis explain to Finn a curiously tempting version of Genesis:

> Where is the man, said Trellis horizontally, that is going to tell me that good can exist side by side with good? Good and evil are complementary terms. You cannot have one without the other. Each gets its force by reason of the other and would be meaningless without the other. There was no good in the Garden till the serpent came, only negation and bathos. Therefore the devil created good. (*MS1* 22)

The explanation of the serpent's function is meant to be conspicuously absurd, but the introductory remarks are salient in their focus on the complementarity of terminology and the "force" established through naming. Here, as in "The Brother Barnabas College Almanac," O'Brien playfully establishes how any word's "meaning" is arrived at through synchronic as well as diachronic forces. To select a word is partially the act of denying other possible words, relegating other possible signifiers to the hidden, darkened wings offstage. And to select a word is to place that word into a variety of interesting tensions with the surrounding networks of syntactical relationships. This emphasis on complementarity, difference, movement, and force not only enables the arcane delineations of the diacritical traits of Mssrs. Furriskey, Lamont, and Shananhan; such a sense of the volatility of language also prompts some of O'Brien's best manuscript revisions.

Returning to a previously mentioned scene, while Orlick takes a break from authoring and saunters off to answer nature's call, Lamont precedes his critical review of Orlick's text with an interesting attention-getting device. The *MS1* typescript originally read: "Lamont extracted a small box from his pocket and proved to the company that it contained but one cigarette; he lit it with the aid of a small machine depending on the combustibility of petroleum gas when mixed with air." (*MS1* 249). The inventive, spurious discourse here proves enchantingly appropriate for the magic show of histrionic gestures. In revising this sentence, however, O'Brien accentuates its qualities of verbal performance. The autograph revisions delight in their own sleight of hand: "Lamont extracted a small box from his pocket *exhibited it* and proved to the company that it contained but one cigarette; he lit *the sole cigarette* with the aid of a small machine depending *for its utility* on the combustibility of petroleum *vapour* when mixed with air" (*MS1* 249 [italics added]).

The first version introduces stylistic inclinations which the revisions enhance. The first commences with a Latinate and legal tone that carries us beyond the simple act of igniting tobacco. The verb "extracted" begins a Latinate "drawing out," which assists the impulse to consciously protract the sentence through scherzando embellishments. The verb "proved" and the phrase "but one cigarette" further the legal tone and elicit the replacement of "it" with "the sole cigarette" which confirms the judicial air. The jurisprudence, however, must compete with an equally compelling tone of hocus-pocus (as is the case with Trellis's trial later on). The "machine" in question seems to possess a curious volition as if it willingly comes to the "aid" of Lamont in his incendiary endeavor. The revision defining this machine (which depends "for its utility on the combustibility of petroleum vapour when mixed with air") casts a spell of scientific precision. The jargon accentuates a series of prepositional phrases which "systematically" refines the description. While reading, we approach an image of a lighter through the pleasures of protracted indirect discourse. Of course, to enhance the artifice, the dull Dutch monosyllable "gas" must be transformed into the more ornate, diffusive "vapour." The selection and arrangement of signs may be likened to the petroleum vapour itself; each is a controlled, explosive mixture. Both operations, lighting a cigarette and configuring words, are touted as *exhibitions of performance*. The sentence, even more than the action it purportedly describes, depends for its pleasure not on utility but on a rococo flair in the execution of its movements.

This sense of verbal performance informs the misleading structure of the novel as the student narrator seeks to establish a presence or self through language. Through a series of biographical reminiscences, we trace his "development" during the formative years, "while the character is receiving its mould" (*AS* 302). The narrator organizes these reminiscences historically, appealing to our predilection for serial arrangements. Emphasizing realistic detail, physical setting, and progressive development, he attempts to invest his "life" with a degree of authenticity. We best appreciate the exorbitance of *At Swim*, however, when we try approaching it with some of the standard critical apparatus for determining meaning. Of course, we find that these tools just miss fitting the nuts and bolts of O'Brien's fiction, but that discovery is itself a starting point in the reexamination of prose fiction and our critical habits of mind.

In "Three Problems of Fictional Form," J. Hillis Miller asks:

> Which is the proper reading of a novel, the first reading when the outcome of the story is in doubt for the reader, so that he is experiencing the events as if they had an open future, like his own life as he lives it, or the second reading when the future is known from the beginning and the full significance of all passages understood as they are encountered?[21]

Miller's question first supposes that we, as readers encountering a novel, identify with a character or characters to the extent that we are absorbed by what happens to so-and-so. And our involvement with the central characters is proportional to the way the events correspond with the temporal processes we have become used to in daily life. The extent to which we are taken in, temporarily treating novelistic events as if they were real, José Ortega y Gasset calls the measure of a book's "imperviousness":

> the author must begin by luring us into the closed precinct that is his novel and then keep us there cut off from any possible retreat to the real space we left behind. . . . The author must build around us a wall without chinks or loopholes through which we might catch, from within the novel, a glimpse of the outside world. For were we allowed to compare the inner world of the book with outer reality and invited to "live," the conflicts, problems, and emotions the book has to offer would seem so small and futile that all their significance would be lost.[22]

Although the outer envelope of *At Swim* presents itself as authentic, O'Brien frequently and deliberately ruptures the "wall" which, in traditional novels, is supposed to keep us contained. We are never more than mildly interested in the fate of the undergraduate narrator. On any reading of the novel, first or fifth, our interest is directed to our dizzying but delightful disorientation. While unsure of our location within the novel's structure, we are always sure that the structure is an artificial construct. The repetitive interruptions of continuity, the conscious sampling of styles, the accent on authoring and rewriting, all help to achieve an effect of purposeful perviousness.

The second half of Miller's question attests to the importance we have learned to ascribe to endings. Usually, we feel freer to engage our critical sensibilities on a second run through a book, when we are not distracted by wondering about the plight of the protagonist. We trust that, by knowing the ending, we are better able to apprehend the shape or form supposedly inherent. A knowledge of the conclusion, we think, should impart new, fuller, or altered significances to the novelistic events which come before. And because temporality predisposes us to think causally, we also tend to view the ending as a product of the events which precede it. This back and forth procedure has become so "natural" for us when we read and reread that we forget the extent to which we use an ending to construct closure, wholeness, and form.

In *At Swim*, the tenth and final biographical reminiscence "neatly" wraps up the college career of the narrator but leaves several more pages of the text unpackaged. The title, "Conclusion of the book antepenultimate," offers a rather conspicuous clue that O'Brien is jostling paradigms of form and function. From the outset, with the emphasis on "three separate openings," he has flaunted his irreverence for traditional approaches to the novel. Here, he flouts our acquired tendency to "find" meaning by approaching from the rear.

Critics often struggle to impose thematic shape onto *At Swim* by reading the final biographical reminiscence as the culmination of the narrator's emotional and social development. Clissmann discovers the narrator learning a "moral lesson" from the proceedings of his "spare-time literary activity": "that imagination is powerful and must not be uncontrolled."[23] Ruth ApRoberts speaks of the narrator finally "finding himself" and attaining an enlightened "benign equilibrium" in terms of resigned maturity.[24] She would have us believe that the uncle's ready congratulations and generous graduation gift awaken the narrator so that "he can now emerge from a pupa stage of adolescent insecurity" into a more mature acceptance of the uncle and his world.[25] And Rudiger Imhof also enjoins this ending with a worn traditional structure: "as in a picaresque novel, the frame-story deals, to some extent, with the development of the principal character from a simpleton to a worldly-wise person (or *Schlem*). It also observes, if liberally, some of the compositional rules of the *Bildungsroman*."[26] Such readings forget that O'Brien has both cheek and tongue and knows very well how to combine the two.

During the course of the novel, the narrator frequently interrupts his recollections to insert an uncomplimentary caricature of
the uncle:

> *Description of my uncle:* Red-faced, bead-eyed, ball-bellied. Fleshy
> about the shoulders with long swinging arms giving ape-like effect to
> gait. Large moustache. Holder of Guinness clerkship the third class.
> (*AS* 11)

> *Description of my uncle:* Rat-brained, cunning, concerned-that-he-
> should-be-well-thought-of. Abounding in pretence, deceit. Holder of
> Guinness clerkship the third class. (*AS* 40)

By the final biographical reminiscence, these descriptions have
become set pieces of ridicule and rebellion. Suddenly, as if overcome with his hearty handshaking acceptance by his uncle and
Mr. Corcoran, the narrator abruptly emends his final presentation:

> *Description of my uncle:* Simple, well-intentioned; pathetic in humility;
> responsible member of large commercial concern. (*AS* 312)

The switch, especially the wording of the job description, is
surely issued with a knowing wink. The narrator's convenient
Joycean epiphany is just as ethereal as the fate of Furriskey and
friends who, in a later ending, go up in smoke "by a curious
coincidence as a matter of fact strange to say" (*AS* 312–13). O'Brien
is flimflamming our sense of an ending, toying with one of the
two basic shapes of the *bildungsroman* in which, according to J.
Hillis Miller, "the attainment of a proper self has often seemed to
coincide with a discovery of place in the community."[27]
The autograph revisions in *MS1* demonstrate that O'Brien deliberately sabotages such traditional propriety. The tame narrative
of a young man developing from adolescent resistance to adult
reconciliation is made more intriguingly feral with several subtle
alterations. The last paragraph of the student narrator's final biographical reminiscence had, at one time, read:

> ~~The Angelus rang out from Haddington Road as~~ I went slowly up the
> stairs to my room. ~~The action~~ my uncle had evinced unsuspected
> traits of ~~contrition~~ character & had induced in me an emotion of
> surprise & contribulice most difficult of literary rendition or descrip-
> tion, ~~& had induced~~ caused my steps to faltered to some extent upon
> the stairs. As I opened my door, my watch told me that the time was 6
> (*MS1* unnumbered leaf "I expressed my thanks")

Then O'Brien made several significant changes which transform the impulses of social integration into a mocking rejection of
the uncle and the world he smugly inhabits. With cross outs,
additions, and a newly-timed punch line, the last paragraph of
this "conclusion" reads:

> I went slowly up the stairs to my room. My uncle had evinced
> unsuspected traits of character & had induced in me an emotion of
> surprise and contribulice most difficult of literary rendition or descrip-
> tion. My steps faltered to some extent upon the stairs. As I opened my
> door, my watch told me that the time was five fifty-four. At the same
> time I heard ~~the peal of~~ the Angelus pealing out from far away,
> perhaps from the Church at Snamh da En or S-t-B. (*MS1* unnumbered
> leaf "I expressed my thanks")

Although impossible to tell exactly when and in what sequence
these changes were made, the revisions distinctly transform the
entire thrust of the passage. In this later version, O'Brien only
teases us with indications of the student narrator's new perspective of acquiescence and acceptance. The act of contrition is
switched from uncle to nephew and our protagonist even his-
trionically stumbles, slowly mounting the stairs, as if overcome by
the error of his previous ways. Instead of the watch reading "6", to
coincide with the church bells calling the community to devo-
tional prayers, the graduation gift now displays its age and de-
bilitation, appropriately slowed (or perhaps even stopped) at five
fifty-four.
All mention of the Angelus is saved for the last sentence punch
line. We are led in the direction of a conventional *bildungsroman*
only to have such a structured whole rigorously lampooned.
When O'Brien switches the location of the Angelus church bells
from Dublin's Haddington Road to the Shannon River's mythic
Snamh-da-En (in English, Swim-Two-Birds), he explodes any traditional shaping that a reader might want to project. O'Brien deletes
this reference to the legendary *Snamh-da-En* in the subsequent
MS2 and in the published novel (no location is mentioned) to
prevent the satire from becoming too obvious. In the published
version, the ending of "Conclusion of the book antepenultimate"
merely mentions that the Angelus is heard "pealing out from far
away," but we might as well be with Sweeny atop a thorny tree if
we want to interpret any layer of this novel with the standard
critical apparatus (*AS* 312).

The Guinness clerkship fun is augmented by the satire of the graduation watch. Together they spoof the narrator's easy contrition and change of heart as they disclose O'Brien's flair for mischief. The watch may be seen as emblematic of the forces from which the narrator has been trying to free himself. A watch represents an agreed-upon, socially authorized means of viewing time. The foundations of community and the institutions it propagates are based on the activity of timepieces like Trellis's "which grappled with each new day as it entered his room . . . from Peter Place, arranging it with precision into twenty-four hours" (*AS* 42). The measurement of duration by stipulated standards (Gregorian calendar, Greenwich meridian) makes possible communal world views as well as narrative conventions of closure. While the watch would be considered an appropriate graduation gift, it is certainly out of place on the person of our narrator. His existence has been a subversive struggle against the established patterns of time. He can no more coordinate his daily habits with the schedule of school than he can accommodate his "spare-time literary activities" to recognizable chronological systems. Just as this writer wreaks vengeance on the usual notions of beginning, middle, and end, he willfully wrestles against integration into the world of the uncle. The banal, conservative, clichéd world of the uncle and Mr. Corcoran remains too confining to support his innovative efforts of expression. It is fitting, then, that the graduation watch "of the second-hand denomination" cannot keep time (*AS* 311).

O'Brien astutely employs the Angelus as a reference point from which to distance his student narrator because the essential spirit of the novel runs counter to this prayer. The Angelus is traditionally rung at morning, noon, and night, calling the community to commemorate the Annunciation. Its name comes from the beginning of the prayer, "Angelus Domini . . ." (The Angel of the Lord . . .), which liturgically commemorates the Incarnation of Christ, the embodiment of God in the human form of Jesus. Theologically, the Annunciation celebrates the achievement of human flesh without the physical interaction of sperm and egg.

The vitality of the novel, however, centers on the ways it demonstrates that you can't make something from nothing. The Incarnation supposedly achieves physical form without the taint of human materials. But O'Brien revels in the physical properties of his material of creation: language. He wants to highlight rather than disavow, the physical sounds, durations, textures, and interactions of words as powerful instruments of invention. Even the comic excursions into "aestho-autogamy" demonstrate how form is determined through various bodies of language. The annunciation of Furriskey's birth is one of many instances where O'Brien dramatizes how styles dictate physical shape:

> We are in position to announce that a happy event has taken place at the Red Swan Hotel, where the proprietor, Mr. Dermot Trellis, has succeeded in encompassing the birth of a man called Furriskey. Stated to be doing "very nicely," the new arrival is about five feet eight inches in height, well-built, dark, and clean shaven. . . . In the course of a brief test conducted by our reporter, he solved a "cut" from an advanced chapter of Hall and Knight's Geometry. . . . Aestho-autogamy with one unknown quantity on the male side, Mr. Trellis told me in conversation, has long been a commonplace. . . . I am very happy to have been fortunate enough to bring a century of ceaseless experiment and endeavor to a triumphant conclusion. (AS 54–55)

Throughout At Swim, O'Brien directs our attention to the physicality of language. All temporary creations take place as ink reconstitutes paper, as style determines form and presence. In the quote above, Furriskey's existence is "encompassed" through society page journalism, mathematics jargon, and linguistic operations of a recognizable medical-science format. In the antepenultimate conclusion of At Swim, our narrator remains "unknown": unencompassed by chronological accuracy, convenient community, or conventions of closure.

Frank Kermode points out that "peripeteia, which has been called the equivalent, in narrative, of irony in rhetoric, is present in every story of the least structural sophistication."[28] Anticipating our novelistic expectations, O'Brien piggybacks irony atop peripeteia as he covertly reverses an apparent reversal. The narrator can not and will not become subject to the confinements inherent in an ignorant acquiescence to methods of expression. His awareness of his linguistic legacy and his enthusiastic appropriation of varieties of styles are a measure of his resistance to—and freedom from—the trappings of the uncle's community. Even while listening to the final lecture on sloth, he catches himself paying most attention to rhetorical patterns:

> Idleness darkens the understanding; idleness weakens the will; idleness leaves you a very good mark for the sinful schemes of the gentleman down below.
> I noticed that in repeating idleness, my uncle had unwittingly utilized a figure of speech usually designed to effect emphasis.

Name of figure of speech: Anaphora (or Epibole). (*AS* 309)

I previously claimed that the primary effect of any reading of *At Swim* is dizzying disorientation. To that I will add that what we remember most about the novel is the narrator's eager, exciting engagement with assorted forms of phrasing. He amuses himself and us by treating language the way a child does Play-Doh modeling clay: he extracts a style, sniffs it, tastes it, rolls it, molds it, stretches it, pokes it—inspecting not only the texture of a particular style, but also the shapes which that style makes possible. The narrator's delightfully wide-eyed attitude towards putting words together obviates any reading of a communal conclusion no matter how critically convenient.

It is precisely this attitude and the focus on "attitudes" as performance which complicate the narrative point of view. As "learned" literary readers, we are accustomed to looking for or constructing ironic distance between the author, the narrator, and the characters of a story. The first-person *bildungsroman* tradition is frequently mined in this manner because it is so grounded in the consequences of a passage of time on the narrator. But *At Swim* does not seem to invite the type of distinctions we are used to making. In fact, O'Brien consciously complicates his fiction by collapsing the differences to which we have become accustomed, narrowing the distance between himself, the autobiographer, and the student.

Throughout the biographical reminiscences, the meticulous attention to details of posture, gesture, and silence attest to the narrator's perception of himself as a self-conscious player striking attitudes. Consider the first sentence of the text: "Having placed in my mouth sufficient bread for three minutes' chewing, I withdrew my powers of sensual perception and retired into the privacy of my mind, *my eyes and face assuming a vacant and preoccupied expression*" (*AS* 9 [italics added]).

At first, we assume that the descriptive adjectives must issue from the mature narrator looking back at his younger self through the agency of memory. But the more we encounter passages such as this, the less certain we are whose voice we are hearing. Both as adolescent and as autobiographer, the narrator is inclined to present himself dramatically. With Brinsley, he often puts on the poor mouth: "Brinsley turned from the window and asked me for a cigarette. I took out my 'butt' or half-spent cigarette and showed it in the hollow of my hand. That is all I have, I said, affecting a pathos in my voice" (*AS* 31). Even when alone he still has a captive audience—himself: "I put the letter with care into a pocket at my right buttock and went to the tender trestle of my bed, arranging my back on it in an indolent horizontal attitude" (*AS* 15).

This self-consciousness of himself as a "player" transgresses the passage of time, collapsing the differences between older and younger sensibilities, blurring the distinctions among O'Brien, the autobiographer, and the student. All "three" approximate one another in the perception of the act of writing as the striking of attitudes in style. In this respect, the final biographical reminiscence can be considered one of several occasions for self-conscious verbal posturings. Having passed his exams, the narrator has earned the opportunity to shake hands with Mr. Corcoran and, most importantly, to "re-present" the activity as variations on a theme. The telling is all:

> How do you do, Mr. Corcoran, I said.
> He arose the better to exert the full force of his fine man-grip. (*AS* 307)

> He arose in a brisk manner and leaning over my uncle's shoulder, caused me to extract my hand from the possession of the latter and present it to him for the exercise of his honest strength. (*AS* 310)

> Looking up, I found that the hand of Mr. Corcoran was extended in an honest manner for the purpose of manual felicitation. (*AS* 311)

Early on, describing his bedroom decor, the narrator furnishes a significant metaphor as he fashions a memorable passage:

> The mirror at which I shaved every second day was of the type supplied gratis by Messrs. Watkins, Jameson and Pim and bore brief letter-press in reference to a proprietary brand of ale between the words of which I had acquired considerable skill in inserting the reflection of my countenance. (*AS* 12)

The image of the undergraduate trying to locate a self within the spatial gaps left by an advertisement is emblematic of the thrust of the entire novel. O'Brien's fiction, including the narrator's "spare-time literary activities," textually documents the never-finished struggle to determine presence between the outlines of established discourses.

3

At Swim-Two-Birds: Verbal Gamesmanship and Palimpsest

> The son of Pharaoh's daughter was the daughter of Pharaoh's son. Know that old one? . . .
> It's all right, as you will see if you work it out with algebra. Let X equal the son of Pharaoh. Go further—call him Mr. X. Then what you have is Mr. X's daughter was the daughter of Mr. X, surely not an unlikely relationship in all the circumstances. . . .
> Don't go yet. There's another way of looking at it. Call Pharaoh's daughter Mrs. Y. Then you have another story—the son of Mrs. Y was Mrs. Y's son. See it?
>
> —Myles na Gopaleen

Self-consciously concocting multiple openings for his "spare-time literary activities," the student narrator (and finally O'Brien) demonstrates his penchant for utilizing a medley of voices. The openings of *At Swim* are significant not so much for their number as for the immediate emphasis on styles as procedures which enable particular shapes.[1] Each opening is introduced in the manner of a leitmotiv: as we encounter characters, we encounter the distinct modes of expression which are the means of their existence. For instance, listen to the first of the "three separate openings":

The Pooka MacPhellimey, a member of the devil class, sat in his hut in the middle of a firwood meditating on the nature of the numerals and segregating in his mind the odd ones from the even. He was seated at his diptych or ancient two-leaved hinged writing-table with inner sides waxed. His rough long-nailed fingers toyed with a snuff-box of perfect rotundity and through a gap in his teeth he whistled a civil cavatina. He was a courtly man and received honour by reason of the generous treatment he gave his wife, one of the Corrigans of Carlow. (*AS* 9)

In this passage, we hear the idiom of provincial, social superiority, a voice pleased with sounding its own prominence. The adjectives "civil" and "courtly" give the Pooka his due, but from a distance. In the appositives "a member of the devil class" and "one of the Corrigans of Carlow," the speaker's voice drops, as if sharing privilege with the listener (after all, the Corrigans of Carlow are "all right" but they're not one of us). We are temporarily drawn into the speaker's circle only to be rebuffed. The condescending explanation of diptych, "or ancient two-leaved hinged writing-table," flaunts the speaker's superior culture and puts us in our place. If only we knew Greek as well as he . . .

O'Brien demands that we read with an ear for what Robert Frost calls "the sound of sense." Frost means that a sentence, as a phonetic unit, has a distinct sound apart from the sounds of the individual words from which it is comprised. He says:

A sentence is a sound in itself on which other sounds called words may be strung. . . .The best place to get the abstract sound of sense is from voices behind a door that cuts off the words. Ask yourself how these sentences would sound without the words in which they are embodied:

You mean to tell me you can't read?
I said no such thing.
Well read then.
You're not my teacher. . . .

One-two-three—go!
No good! Come back—come back.
Haslam go down there and make those kids get out of the track.

Those sounds are summoned by the audile [audial] imagination and they must be positive, strong, and definitely and unmistakeably indicated by the context. The reader must be at no loss to give his voice the posture proper to the sentence.[2]

Reading *At Swim*, we are asked to recognize—in some cases we are taught to recognize—distinct sentence sounds, hearing the intonations and cadences which help compose a style. An appreciation of the novel depends on our hearing the way particular voices are appropriated, innovatively modified, and given the opportunity to contend with other voices. The novel explores how these sound-shapes fare against one another and against time. Later in the text, for instance, the Pooka appropriates this "social" voice through which he acquired existence and, in a memorable scene, urbanely sounds off a number of other voices during the visit to Orlick's nativity. And a similar set of "mannered" sentence sounds informs the tea scene during "a social evening at the Furriskey household" when a ceremoniously civil style of address attempts—and comically fails—to steer the conversation clear of uncouth considerations such as blackheads, boils, and bedsores.

I will be returning to an examination of how the sound of sense operates in the novel, but for now I want to stress that, because O'Brien hears sounds so well, it is impossible for him to consider words as fixed entities which express a stable content. He evinces above all a fascination with styles as phonetic systems of relationship. In coming to terms with the vast legacy of language, he discovers that his inheritance may be viewed as much as an enabling condition as an inhibiting restraint.

The narrator obviously appreciates, as both performer and spectator, the display of his prowess of tongue and pen. While his linguistic efforts sometimes exude an "undergraduate" flavor, they illustrate a significant, healthy attitude toward language—an attitude which enables the fun of the "spare-time literary activity" and, by extension, the fun of *At Swim-Two-Birds.*

Through the narrator, O'Brien treats language as an experience to be taken advantage of. Listening to himself in the process of composition, he seeks the opportunity of handling new words and renewing those with which we assume we are familiar. In all of the wordplay of the novel, however, O'Brien questions the extent to which one can control by naming.

Most of us can recall (often with embarrassment) the first time we *heard* a word we *thought* we knew *already.* Usually, we had been reading the word for years and could confidently define it, but since we had never heard the word spoken, it never truly existed as an aural experience. One day, by chance, often in response to our most humbling error, we hear the word pronounced correctly for the first time. Suddenly, almost magically, the word we thought we knew is transformed into a new entity with a novel phonetic signature. Inevitably, we find the occasions—as if atoning for past sins—to use our new possession in conversation at least eleven times that week. Or we discover by means of a crossword clue or an interesting friend, a new variation in a species we thought complete. Again, the new addition to our vocabulary becomes a possession with our title to it seemingly reinforced every time we pronounce the word. We like to hear ourselves sounding the word, running our tongue over every facet, experimenting with the subtle actions it performs on various sentences. Just the sound of our new word may call forth similar (or antithetical) sounds and thus exert a shaping influence. We find it dictating a climate of vocabulary for which we were unprepared, or creating a motion in a sentence with which we enjoy trying to keep up.

These are the types of experience which generate the narrator's verbal gamesmanship. *At Swim* exhibits the excitement of listening to oneself employ words before they become hard and stale, before their sounds become unrecognized background, before their ability to "mean" becomes dessicated by routine. The novel documents the narrator's—and O'Brien's—delight in canvassing the texture of words and the variety of procedures by which they might be arranged.

As I mentioned previously, the narrator frequently interrupts his reminiscences to demonstrate his awareness of rhetorical procedures. In response to Kelly's suggestion that they drink a few "jars," the narrator explains:

> I derived considerable pleasure from the casual quality of his suggestion and observed that it would probably do us no harm, thus expressing my whole-hearted concurrence by a figure of speech.

> *Name of figure of speech:* Litotes (or Meiosis). (*AS* 26)

The passage exemplifies the way the narrator attends to his own and others' language as it is being issued. His self-consciousness about linguistic procedures urges him to explore the structures of consciousness by which we make sense of the world, considering such structures as systems with which one might creatively negotiate. In Kelly's choice of the colloquial "jars" (almost the equivalent of "pints"), the narrator hears the voice of drinking camaraderie and acceptance. Although uninitiated into the pleasures and perils of intoxicating beverage, our storymaker affects an air of nonchalance with his arrangement of words. His self-conscious understatement is meant to conceal his excitement and anxiety beneath the mask of extensive pub experience. Significantly, he is most pleased with his ability to name the trope he uses, flaunting a familiarity with systems of formal rhetoric in the tradition of Quintilian and Puttenham.

As a side note, I suspect that O'Brien may be smiling at the ironic inappropriateness of scholarly training for the undergraduate's first efforts in Grogan's pub. Explaining "litotes," Puttenham says, "We temper our sense with words of such moderation as in appearance to abateth it, but not in deed."[3] The moderation displayed in the choice of words contrasts with the subsequent immoderate experience with a "mass of plain porter," and the narrator's expression that such an evening "would do us no harm" turns on him. He tempers his sense to the point of distemper, suffering the digestive consequences of the porter's toxic content.

In naming the tropes he uses, the narrator deliberately provides both the Latin and Greek terminology. He delights in exhibiting his scholastic knowledge of the classical languages and gets a great charge out of tossing off Latin clichés in the company of his uncle, who inevitably agrees without comprehending. This joking around, however, reveals a stance which is more than frivolous.

To impress the members of Michael Byrne's little salon, the undergraduate finds himself improvising on his script. In a moment of inspired, dreadful punning, he constructs two extraneous characters to threaten the stability of the plot. Shanahan and Lamont are almost shanghaied by "two decadent Greek scullions, Timothy Danaos and Dona Ferentes, ashore from the cooking galley of a strange ship" (AS 142). The narrator derives considerable pleasure from the demonstration of his wit without giving it much thought, but the punning deserves consideration as an indication of a particular "feel" for language. The Greek sailors' names recall an oft quoted passage from Vergil's *Aeneid*. Voicing his suspicion of the Trojan horse, Laocoon exclaims, "*timeo Danaos et dona ferentes*" ("I fear the Greeks even when they offer gifts"). So we have an inside joke to be shared by those familiar with the *Aeneid* as a Latin class translation exercise. But, more importantly, we have an indication that O'Brien is toying with some of the more interesting notions which contemporary critics have staked off as their domain.

First, the joking indicates a willingness to consider the sound of a word apart from its meaning. As vocal emanations from the larynx, the sounds "timeo Danaos" have no *necessary* relationship with the concept "I fear the Greeks," just as the sound of the word "Greeks" has no *necessary* relationship with the people who populate an Aegean peninsula. Without any conscious formulation of linguistic theory, the narrator shows a sense that all language has an existence as it is transmitted vocally, which differs, or is apart, from its existence as a system of signs for items or concepts. It is one thing to read Latin and translate it into English (as if Danaos = Greeks), but the narrator evinces a more interesting habit of mind by appropriating just the sounds of words and then constructing with them. Saussure would say that he is attempting to separate the signifier from the signified; I prefer to say that he is exploring the extremely tenuous relationship between the "sound-texture" and "concept" of signs.[4]

This method of viewing his literary inheritance evinces a healthy disrespect for the established systems of coherence which authorize "meaning." Laocoon's warning depends on the perception of his words in time, as they relate to one another diachronically. In the phrase, "timeo Danaos et dona ferentes," the meaning takes shape as each word follows another and it is not complete until the final word has been realized. To appropriate the phonetic sounds of "timeo Danaos," and to use these aural vibrations to construct the "name" of a foreign unsavory, explodes the system of coherence through which Laocoon's message derives its meaning.

To be sure, the humor of the pun depends on its perception without weighty analysis: it is absurd, it is extravagant, but most of all it is having a good time with sounds. The Irish, of course, have traditionally demonstrated a flair for pun-fun, with Joyce, arguably, the preeminent player in the twentieth century. In this instance, however, I believe that O'Brien is referring more to the Latino-Angelicus games developed by Jonathan Swift and Dr. Thomas Sheridan than to Joyce. As Vivian Mercier points out, Swift and Sheridan frequently wrote letters to each other in which English was to be read as Latin and vice versa. One of Swift's letters begins, "Am I say vain a Rabble is" which should be read, *"Amice venerabilis."* In another letter, with perhaps more wit, Sheridan reverses the process; he writes, *"Mi mollis ab uti, an angeli se. An has fine iis, a fine face, ab re ast as no, a belli fora que en. Andi me quis mi mollis as I pleas."* With a little practice, this can be seen as "My Molly's a beauty, an angel, I say. And has fine eyes, a fine face, a breast as snow, a belly for a queen. And I may kiss (quiz?) my Molly as I please."[5]

Whether writing newspapers or novels, O'Brien never lost his ear for aural games. As late as 1965, the year before his death, he exhibits an attitude akin with his youthful narrator's. Reviewing the book *George Bernard Shaw on Language* by Abraham Tauber, he gravitates, as might be expected, to a discussion of Shaw's project for a phonetically consistent alphabet. With the greatest admiration for verbal sport, O'Brien informs us: "Over the years, he [Shaw] spent much time and work in setting up a cockshot to look smart in knocking it down. An early wisecrack of his was the word 'fish,' spelt 'ghoti'—the 'gh' of 'laugh,' the 'o' of 'women,' and the 'ti' of 'nation.' "[6]

In addition to his own wisecracking, the narrator of *At Swim* evinces an attraction for erudite, arcane words which exist outside the mainstream of conversation and probably beyond the scope of most reading. Like many of Samuel Beckett's characters, he loves the out-of-the-way words, the ones which might be gleaned from the most demanding crossword puzzles. These he stores "in the odd corners of my mind," on standby alert, reserved for propitious occasions. At one point, Brinsley objects to the depiction of Furriskey, Lamont, and Shanahan, claiming that they are not sufficiently distinct to be awarded separate identities. Pretending to be genuinely concerned with "characterization in contemporary literary works of a high-class, advanced or literary nature," the narrator defends their dissimilarity, mustering his reserves for combat:

> Your objections are superficial, I responded. These gentlemen may look the same and speak the same but actually they are profoundly dissimilar. For example, Mr. Furriskey is of the brachycephalic order, Mr. Shanahan of the prognathic.
> Prognathic? (*AS* 230–31)

He thoroughly enjoys maneuvering with his new words, savoring their sounds as well as their ability to determine difference. The pleasures of "brachycephalic" depend as much on the sounding of five syllables as on an academic awareness of Greek roots. He is having fun, the way we all do, trying out strange words: listening to them, hearing how they sound during different occasions, appreciating the nuances of cadence and connotation, gauging their effects on audiences. The result of this indulgence is a document which systematically refutes Brinsley's proposition:

> *Memorandum of the respective diacritical traits or qualities of Messrs. Furriskey, Lamont and Shanahan:*
>
> Head: brachycephalic; bullet; prognathic.
> Vision: tendencies toward myopia; wall-eye; nyctalopia.
> Configuration of the nose: roman; snub; mastoid.
> Unimportant physical afflictions: palpebral ptosis; indigestion; German itch.
> Mannerisms: tendency to agitate or flick fingers together in prim fashion after conveying bread or other crumbling substance to

mouth; tooth-sucking and handling of tie-knot; ear-poking with pin
or match, lip-pursing.
Outer clothing: D.B. indigo worsted; S.B. brown serge, two button
style; do., three button style.
Inner or under-clothing: woollen combinations, front buttoning style;
home-made under-tabard of stout moreen-cloth (winter) or para-
matta (summer); abdominal belt or corset with attached unguinal
protective appliance. (*AS* 231)

Poor Shanahan. If we reconstruct him from the terminology
which names his traits, we find that: his jaw juts forward, he can't
see at night, his nose is shaped like a breast, his ears obviously
need cleaning, and he must triumph over the elasticity of his truss
to scratch vital areas.

The narrator surely speaks for O'Brien when he pleads guilty to
consulting "standard works of reference" (*AS* 231). Anyone at-
tuned to O'Brien's sensibility can't help but picture him gleefully
thumbing through medical texts, dictionaries, thesauri, and gar-
ment catalogues, pirating the strangest terminology and constructing a most bizarre "systematic" memorandum which
parodies the arbitrariness of all systems.

Because the memorandum ruptures the usual temporal format
of language, it also subtly explores the way words operate vertically, or synchronically. Because language exists and is perceived
in time, we usually read and speak horizontally, establishing the
meaning in terms of sequential, or diachronic, relationship. In the
sentence, "Furriskey's head is brachycephalic," the meaning arrives as we make our way through the characters from capital "F"
to the period. The meaning of each word depends on its position
in the sentence and its syntactical relationship with other words
which come before and after. But O'Brien is calling attention to
the way a word is also defined vertically, by its difference from a
range of words which might have been, but were not, chosen at
that time. "Brachycephalic," then, is given shape by the absence
of other words. Furriskey's head is brachycephalic, not prog-
nathic, not bullet, not oblong, not oval. This set of possible choices
(all referring to shape) is defined by its diacritical relationship
with other possible sets or systems, each with its own environment or coherence. Furriskey's head is brachycephalic, not cold,
not flushed, not sweaty; nor is it neatly combed, widow-peaked,
or tonsured. The memorandum prompts closer thinking about
words and the operations they perform. For O'Brien, the pleasures of utilizing language are most readily realized when one

savors the mechanisms by which a mode of discourse defines itself.

The reflexivity of language incidentally informs one of the narrator's affiliated interests. I am thinking of his penchant for introducing an indistinct "noise" so that he may employ various linguistic procedures to circumscribe its boundaries. For me, the most provocative oddities occur when he uses metaphor to "define" noises. In response to the narrator's Timothy Danaos and Dona Ferentes piece, "Byrne made a noise in the darkness of a kind associated with the forcible opening of the lid of a tin container" (AS 143). After Mr. Corcoran suffers the consequences of an unexpected sneeze, the narrator plays Hamlet scrutinizing Yorick's skull: "As my uncle hurried to his assistance, I felt that my gorge was about to rise. I retched slightly, making a noise with my throat similar to that utilized by persons in the article of death" (AS 133).

I. A. Richards is most helpful when he says of metaphor: "It is the supreme agent by which disparate and hitherto unconnected things are brought together in poetry for the sake of the effects upon attitude and impulse which spring from their collocation and from the combinations which the mind then establishes between them."[7] These passages act to urge our imaginative colloquy; there is something unusual going on here which elicits an attitude of healthy inquisitiveness. Unlike some of the rude noises soon to be examined, these sounds cannot easily be labeled by a name and must be approximated by a process of equivalence.

But the relationship between the subject, in each case "noise," and its metaphoric substitute is not one of "equivalence"; it is much more tenuous than that. One noise is "of a kind associated with" a particular aural impression and the other noise is "similar to" another sound wave pattern. So the most we can say is that these noises exist somewhere *near* their replacements; they share some of the same qualities, but beyond that, the definition weakens. And what about the standards of comparison? What sound does the lid of a tin container emit when forcibly opened? What sound do people utilize "in the article of death?" Since the sounds in question only obliquely correspond with a visual image, we are left with what Robert Frost calls the "audile imagination." If we can't recall the experience of these sounds directly (I can't. How much force is "forcibly"? Which article is "the article of death?"), we must imaginatively construct synonymous situations. We think: "the tin container sound probably resembles *this*" (another noise) or "a dying person might sound like *this*" (another aural substitute). To return to the passage from Richards, the effect of these constructs is to draw us deeper into the game. Our impulse is to domesticate the strange metaphors, attempting to stabilize by calling on more words. Hopefully, inevitably returning to our point of departure, we begin to ponder the degree to which the thinking process itself is metaphoric. Ideally, we begin to consider metaphor, not as a figure of speech learned in grammar school, but as a "supreme agent" which fundamentally informs patterns of consciousness.

While the structure and learned wit of *At Swim* recall that of Laurence Sterne's *Tristram Shandy* and Rabelais's *Gargantua and Pantagruel*, the fascination with rhetorical procedures and figures of speech is similar to that exhibited in Sir Philip Sidney's *Arcadia*. For O'Brien as well as Sidney, the plot of a narrative is of secondary importance, acting as a vehicle for the display of inventive prose and stylistic eloquence. In reference to the *Arcadia*, Maurice Evans says: "The Elizabethan liked his nature embellished by art, provided that the two worked in harmony with each other, and he felt none of the automatic distrust of artifice in itself which is a feature of romantic and modern taste."[8]

The similarities between O'Brien and Sidney are nowhere more apparent than in their fondness for periphrasis. In his *Directions for Speech and Style* (1599), John Hoskins tries to account for the pleasure derived from periphrasis:

> It cannot be but if either the meaning or the words be obscure or unfamiliar unto a man's mind, that the speech so consisting should be much accepted; and yet it is impossible that there should be any extraordinary delight in ordinary words and plain meaning. How then shall we determine? It is as it is in many dishes at our table: our eyes and taste give them commendation, nor for the substance but for the dressing and service.[9]

Hoskins cites several examples from the *Arcadia*, demonstrating periphrasis's ability to utilize everyday words for extraordinary effect: "Instead of 'his name was known to high and low,' he [Sidney] saith that 'no prince could pretend height nor beggar lowness to bar him from the sounds thereof.' For 'old and young malcontents,' he saith: 'such whom youthful age or youthful minds had filled with unlimited desires.' "[10]

In the *Arcadia*, Sidney uses periphrasis to heighten and intensify "normal human responses," imparting a decorative effect appropriate for the noble stature of the characters.[11] In *At Swim*, however, O'Brien enhances the "dressing and service" of meals unfit for consumption. During the narrator's pub apprenticeship, he learns his limit the hard way:

> I proceeded home one evening in October after leaving a gallon of half-digested porter on the floor of a public-house in Parnell Street and put myself with considerable difficulty into bed, where I remained for three days on the pretence of a chill. I was compelled to secrete my suit beneath the mattress because it was offensive to at least two of the senses and bore an explanation of my illness contrary to that already advanced.
>
> *The two senses referred to:* Vision, smell. (*AS* 29–30)

Here, the elegant parlance of the passage contends with our natural human response of repugnance, somehow eliciting a smile. The precision of details—the amount of his outburst, its alimentary condition, the location of the tragedy—together with the circuitous route by which he explains his insufficient trajectory deceive the ear and create a jocose inversion of propriety. The periphrastic style places the reader at a safe distance from which to appreciate the difference between what is expressed and what is meant.

O'Brien is "characteristically Irish" in his attention to human metabolic ceremonies acquired through the agency of Adam's Fall. Anyone familiar with even the standard Irish works pinched by anthologists of "English" literature must realize that the Irish exhibit an unusual interest in the excretory processes by which the body governs its health. Stephen Dedalus never quite recovers from being shouldered into "the square ditch" and grows to confuse sexuality with obscenity. In Lilliput, Gulliver extinguishes a fire in the imperial place by voiding a copious amount of wine-induced urine, and, in the land of the Houyhnhnms, he is abased by the Yahoos who leap into trees and discharge their feces on his head. Thomas Kinsella points out that such a scatological interest antedates the advent of the English language in Ireland; ancient Irish literature conventionally and openly accommodates matters we might think coarse or crude. Kinsella states: "A strong element in the sagas is their directness in bodily matters: the easy references to seduction, copulation, urination, the picking of vermin."[12]

One example of this tradition occurs at the conclusion of the *Táin Bó Cuailnge* (*The Cattle-Raid of Cualnge*) when Cúchulainn spares the life of his enemy Queen Medb, partly because she is indisposed:

> Then Medb got her gush of blood.
> "Fergus," she said, "take over the shelter of shields at the rear of the men of Ireland until I relieve myself."
> "By god," Fergus said, "you have picked a bad time for this."
> "I can't help it," Medb said. "I'll die if I can't do it."
> So Fergus took over the shelter of shields at the rear of the men of Ireland and Medb relieved herself. It dug three great channels, each big enough to take a household. The place is called Fual Medba, Medb's Foul Place, ever since. Cúchulainn found her like this but he held his hand. He wouldn't strike her from behind.[13]

O'Brien appropriates the Irish scatological tradition but transforms it by using it as an occasion for various periphrastic feats of verbal dexterity. He introduces such matters to compete with conventions by improvising with oblique references. Eschewing the direct approach, he prefers to experiment with various means of naming without naming.

At one point, in reference to the ill effects of alcoholic indulgence, the narrator explains, "I opened wide my windpipe and made a coarse noise unassociated with the usages of gentlemen" (*AS* 30). Such a passage charms his audience and prompts us to wonder how such a performance compares with, say, that of Sir Toby Belch in *Twelfth Night*. Viewing Shakespeare's play, we expect Toby to assault the ears (especially Malvolio's) with esophogeal sounds which might be written "ruupt." We are once removed from the experience of the sound when we name it a "burp" or a "belch," but the narrator's elaborate construct removes us even further. We are not involved with social manners so much as the manner of this description. The careful placement of the word "wide," the alliteration of *w*'s, the consonance of *d*'s, *p*'s, and *s*'s, and the backdoor action of the final phrase, which almost reverses the metaphoric process, accentuate the sentence as a willful, willfully artificial invention.

The narrator's casual fun implicitly calls into question the nature of signs. His description of a gastric disturbance urges us to pause and reconsider how words operate. Here, one signifier or word-image "burp" has been replaced by an oblique arrangement of fifteen approximations. The arrangement parades its ingenuity and, while it remains a signifier (for the type of sound we expect from Sir Toby), it assumes the status of a signified or concept in its own right.

The sport, of course, is to name the unnamable; since it is an old game, the contest for innovation becomes more difficult the more it is played. Polite practice and the expansion of plumbing dictate that certain words, like the functions they represent, be channeled underground. The narrator adopts the guise of punctilio to satirize society's whims and, simultaneously, to improvise on the Irish convention of direct reference (current in James Joyce's "cloacal obsession").

All of the word-games in the novel are intended to arouse us from any semisomnolent imperceptions of language. Everyday conversation, newspaper reports, and the traditional novel employ words so routinely that they efface themselves as means and processes. By using exorbitant words, or common words in exorbitant arrangements, the narrator urges us to look *at* words rather than to assume we are looking *through* them. Too often, we treat language as if it were a transparent medium, a window through which we see "things." O'Brien's eccentric selection and combination of words demand that we conceive of language as an opaque, textured instrument of invention.

Like many modernists, O'Brien investigates how words might be "made strange" to us through speaking and writing. Unless we become cognizant of language as form and process, we fail to realize the ways that structures of discourse inform all our perceptions: our way of "seeing" the novel, ourselves, and the world in which we live. As Terence Hawkes points out, when language becomes too familiar, we become "anaesthetized to its distinctive features" and to its ability to shape thought.[14] According to the Russian Formalists, "the aim of poetry is to reverse that process, to defamiliarize that with which we are overly familiar, to 'creatively deform' the usual, the normal, and so to inculcate a new, child-like, non-jaded vision in us."[15]

In this sense, the narrator of *At Swim* uses words poetically. Language is not designed to communicate information so much as it is designed to call attention to itself as an activity. *At Swim* canvasses the texture of words and the variety of systems by which they might be combined, emphasizing the role of fiction as creative distortion. O'Brien's use of language resembles the volute of an Ionic capital which turns in on itself. The volute is hardly necessary in terms of architectural support—a plain, unadorned column would keep up the roof—but the volute confers a special aesthetic pleasure precisely because its "support" of the edifice transcends utility.

In terms of "the sound of sense," we aurally recognize and can place almost all of the styles employed in *At Swim* from the "objective," sober, matter-of-fact newspaper extracts to the "chap-slappin', hell-bent-for-leather, sixgun-totin' jargon" of Shorty Andrews. But unless the reader is familiar with the medieval traditions of Irish literature, the Finn MacCool and Mad Sweeny sections might pose a problem. V. S. Pritchett, who calls *At Swim* a "brilliant and wicked book," has difficulty with the Finn passages, claiming that Finn's adventures "get rather boring."[16] Most readers, however, have more trouble maintaining interest in the staves of Sweeny. I suspect that the difficulty arises from our disorientation and the novelistic desire to "get on with it," through (and back) to styles with which we are more at home. Once we begin to savor sounds, however, we discover that Finn and Sweeny are, to use Pritchett's phrase, "splendid taken a page at a time."[17] As O'Brien teaches us to recognize their techniques of delivery, we begin to appreciate his flair for smuggling these techniques into his own storytelling.

We are introduced to Finn MacCool on the second page of the novel as a "legendary hero of old Ireland," supposedly the same warrior/hunter Finn MacCumhall who led the Fianna in the days before St. Patrick made his debut. In *The Ossianic Lore and Romantic Tales of Medieval Ireland,* Gerard Murphy explains that the twelfth century composition *Acallam na Senorach (The Colloquy of the Ancient Men)* transformed Finn from an ancillary folktale figure into one of the most prominent literary legends:

> Up to the twelfth century . . . Fionn, though clearly well known in Irish tradition, had held no important place in the narrative lore of the *filidh*. By the end of that century, however, Fionn and his Fiana had advanced well on their way towards that preeminent position which was ultimately to be theirs.[18]

The reasons for this metamorphosis are many; in essence, however, Finn became an epic figure because the tales of his exploits were consciously embellished and augmented. Professor Murphy explains: "His cycle was . . . eminently suited for further development at the hands of learned storytellers in accordance with the progressive spirit of the century."[19] As one of the most learned storytellers of our century, O'Brien develops the Finn tradition most peculiarly, accommodating the "progressive spirit" of the twelfth century to the comic spirit of *At Swim.*

In 1892, Standish Hayes O'Grady made the Finn cycle accessible to the majority of Irishmen who had not yet learned their own language. From a variety of manuscripts in the British Museum and the Royal Irish Academy, O'Grady revived many forgotten myths, sagas, and legends, including the tales of Finn and his Fianna. Flann O'Brien had the greatest admiration for O'Grady, lauding him as much for his innovative invention as for his meticulous scholarship. Less than a year after publishing *At Swim*, O'Brien wrote an article for the *Irish Times*, commending O'Grady's "gift of combining the real stuff of scholarship with his own irrepressible breeziness. . . . His originality and agility of mind bubble up in the prefaces to his works and are reflected in the curious and charming English which he devised in an effort to render to the student the last glint of colour in any Irish word."[20]

O'Brien certainly knew O'Grady's *Silva Gadelica* intimately. He probably borrowed from it when composing *At Swim*, but most importantly, applied his own brand of breeziness to the modes of expression it authorized. Compare the accounts of qualification for the Fianna. First O'Grady's version:

> Of all these again, not a man was taken until he were a prime poet versed in the twelve books of poesy. No man was taken till in the ground a large hole had been made (such as to reach the fold of his belt) and he put into it with his shield and a forearm's length of a hazel stick. Then must nine warriors, having nine spears, with a ten-furrows' width betwixt them and him, assail him and in concert let fly at him. If past that guard of his he were hurt then, he was not received into Fianship. Not a man of them was taken till his hair had been interwoven into braids on him and he started at a run through Ireland's woods; while they, seeking to wound him, followed in his wake, there having been between him and them but one forest bough by way of interval at first. Should he be overtaken, he was wounded and not received into the Fianna after.[21]

Now O'Brien's:

> Till a man has accomplished twelve books of poetry, the same is not taken for want of poetry but is forced away. No man is taken till a black hole is hollowed in the world to the depth of his two oxters and he put into it to gaze from it with his lonely head and nothing to him but his shield and a stick of hazel. Then must nine warriors fly their spears at him, one with the other and together. If he be spear-holed past his shield, or spear-killed, he is not taken for want of shield skill. No man is taken till he is run by warriors through the woods of Erin with his hair bunched-loose about him for bough-tangle and briar-twitch. Should branches disturb his hair or pull it forth like sheep-wool on a hawthorn, he is not taken but is caught and gashed. (*AS* 20–21)

It looks as if O'Brien treats *Silva Gadelica* the same way his under-graduate does the *Conspectus of the Arts and Natural Sciences:* "Opening it, I read a passage which I subsequently embodied in my manuscript as being suitable for my purpose" (*AS* 40). How-ever, one can never be sure of O'Brien's sources; he was an excellent Gaelic scholar himself and had access to a copy of the rendition from which O'Grady worked.[22] But if, as is likely, O'Brien "embodied" a passage directly from O'Grady's transla-tion, he made subtle but significant modifications which indicate his own "originality and agility of mind."

In comparison with O'Grady's, O'Brien's account is "made stranger" to us through his decisions of syntax and diction. The first sentences especially demonstrate that O'Grady's version ac-commodates itself to the usual syntactical patterns of English in a way that O'Brien's doesn't. O'Brien also chooses to employ hy-phenated constructs with which we are least familiar; instead of the hair being "interwoven into braids," it is "bunched-loose," a less precise and more intriguing arrangement. But, more sug-gestively, O'Brien's passage is pregnant with a phoenetic empha-sis which we associate with the conventions of oral tradition. Even if the reader has never heard of Finn, O'Brien makes these sections sound older, more distant, belonging to a tradition of recitation rather than reading. The alliteration is most conspic-uous; in the second sentence alone we encounter eight aspirating *h*'s: "hole," "hollowed," "he," "his," "head," "him," "his," "hazel." Assonance, too, makes its presence felt in such patterns as "gaze," "hazel," and "killed," "skilled." We also hear entire words re-peated frequently, oscillating in function between nouns and ad-jectives: "spear," and "spear-killed," "shield" and "shield-skill."

In O'Brien's passage, one has more of a sense of ancient incan-tation with certain sounds *calling forth* neighboring sounds. As Vivian Mercier explains, such repetitions are a fundamental pro-cedure of oral verbal magic:

> Word play in its other sense—play with words—is an important element of the Old Irish spells and incantations. . . . Indeed, word play is so prevalent in all verbal magic that it is summed up in the popular expression "hocus-pocus" which reproduces neatly the kind of jingle common in spells and in the modern nursery rhymes appar-ently derived from them.[23]

In *The Irish Tradition*, Robin Flower recounts his own experience with verbal magic, an experience not unlike listening to Finn.

Earlier this century, out for a stroll in the West of Ireland, Flower encountered a potato digger "of over eighty years," who welcomed the chance meeting as an opportunity to rest his spade and exercise his tongue:

> After a little while he changed from poetry to prose and began to recite a long tale of Fionn and his companions and their adventures throughout the world, how they came to Greece and what strange things befell them there. At times, the voice would alter and quicken, the eyes would brighten, as with a speed which you would have thought beyond the compass of human breath he delivered those highly artificial passages describing a fight or a putting out to sea, full of strange words and alliterating rhetorical phrases which, from the traditional hurried manner of narration, are known as "runs." At the end of one of these he would check a moment with his eye, draw a deep breath, and embark once more on the level course of his recitation.
> I listened spellbound.[24]

Most significantly, when O'Brien helps to recover a tradition by employing it in his novel, he covers it with his own peculiar magic. First he plays with and augments the features of the Finn style which he is "re-creating." Then he appropriates and exploits this bardic mode of delivery, applying it in comically incongruous situations, such as Brinsley's "tour de force . . . description [of Trellis] in the Finn canon" (AS 35). Ultimately, through parody, O'Brien hopes to reanimate a host of particular styles as well as the novel as a genre.

While O'Brien begins by following O'Grady's lead, he moves off on his own just as soon as he has established a conducive set of steps. The description of Finn becomes an opportunity to flex his linguistic muscles:

> The neck to him was as the bole of a great oak, knotted and seized together with muscle-humps and carbuncles of tangled sinew. . . . The chest to him was wider than the poles of a good chariot, coming now out, now in, and pastured from chin to navel with meadows of black man-hair and meated with layers of fine man-meat. . . . The arms to him were like the necks of beasts, ball-swollen with their bunched-up brawnstrings and blood-veins, the better for harping and hunting and contending with the bards. (AS 17–18)

The traditional repetition of sound and epic exaggeration are themselves exaggerated as the prose seems to swell itself with marvelous metaphors. O'Brien has set up a type of discursive activity and invites us to explore its resources. But, from the beginning, we are never allowed to listen with a straight face. The Finn canon is one of the several occasions O'Brien has arranged in order to have his way with words. With each description attempting to outdo its predecessor, the prose seems to acquire a momentum of its own. Before long, we find Finn and, more significantly, the means of his telling, careening into the arena of comic burlesque:

> Three fifties of fosterlings could engage with handball against the wideness of his backside, which was wide enough to halt the march of warriors through a mountain-pass. . . . The knees and calves to him, swealed and swathed with soogawns and Thomond weed-ropes, were smutted with dungs and dirt-daubs of every hue and pigment, hardened by stainings of mead and trickles of metheglin and all the dribblings and drippings of his medher, for it was the custom of Finn to drink nightly with his people. (*AS* 18–19)

O'Brien is not so much making fun of what was once a heroic tradition as he is making fun with the conventional verbal possibilities he is "re-creating."

Vivian Mercier claims that a distinctive characteristic of "the Gaelic comic genius" is his [i.e., the Gaelic comic genius without regard to gender] ambivalent view of his archaic heritage: "Like Homer or Aristophanes, he seems to believe in myth and magic with one half of his being, while with the other half he delights in their absurdity."[25] Although a familiarity with Irish literary heritage enhances the appreciation of *At Swim*, it is by no means a prerequisite for participating in O'Brien's fun. The reader quickly learns to recognize a particular set of phonetic repetitions, syntactical arrangements, and cadences as "belonging to" Finn Mac-Cool. But just as one begins to feel comfortable identifying and locating certain verbal configurations as bardic, he finds this strange stylistic animal forsaking his "proper" habitat and wandering into environments created by other styles.

When the author Dermot Trellis is first being invented, the undergraduate describes his "average stature," prickly-heated flab, and barometric pimples in the blandest, pseudonovelistic, subject-verb-object prose: "He was voluntarily bedridden and suffered from no organic or other illness. He occasionally rose for very brief periods in the evening to pad about the empty house in his felt slippers . . ." (*AS* 34). Suddenly, Brinsley dissolves this Trellis and "re-forms" him in a Finn-like, bardic/heroic manner:

The neck to Trellis is house-thick and house-rough and is guarded by night and day against the coming of enemies by his old watchful boil. His bottom is the stern of a sea-blue schooner, his stomach is its mainsail with a filling of wind. His face is a snowfall on old mountains, the feet are fields. (*AS* 35)

A bit later, Trellis is once again recontrived, this time in the mold of a "Doctor Beatty (now with God)," the prepositional style having been provided by the twenty-first volume of *A Conspectus of the Arts and Natural Sciences:* "In person he was of the middle size, of a broad square make, which seemed to indicate a more robust constitution than he really possessed. In his gait, there was something of a slouch. During his later years he grew corpulent and unwieldy . . ." (*AS* 40).

The effect of such a procedure—and rewriting is the central activity of the novel—resembles the experience of optical refraction and displacement. This optical phenomenon occurs when a long, straight object, say a straw, is placed in a half-full glass of water. If one views the structure from the side, the straw seems to bend a bit as it enters the glass, then bend more noticeably as it proceeds through the water. In order to complicate the scientific model—as O'Brien surely would—float a little clear oil on top of the water and the straw seems to bend again. (Young children are more likely to notice such things as their eyes are level with countertops and tables. They're not above looking sideways.) Whether six or fifty-six, however, one ought to wonder how and why a straight straw is magically made crooked. Any standard physics textbook explains that, relative to our position, light waves travel at different speeds as they make their way through air, glass, oil, water. The optical displacement is a product of refraction—the deflection of light waves at the boundaries between different media.

The magic of *At Swim* is the discovery that refraction and displacement occur in any discourse, in all modes of expression. Dermot Trellis is "bent" several ways as his person is passed through several styles. The procedure is pushed to an intriguing extreme once Orlick, Furriskey, Shanahan, and Lamont decide to take turns authoring the author. Recommending that the "wonders" are to be glimpsed by looking sideways at language, O'Brien frequently plays with the contorting disposition of discourse in a way similar to Thomas Pynchon. In *The Crying of Lot 49*, Mucho Maas interviews his wife Oedipa Maas from the mobile broadcast booth of KCUF. He concludes his questioning:

"Thank you, Mrs. Edna Mosh . . ."

"Edna Mosh?" Oedipa said.

"It'll come out the right way," Mucho said. "I was allowing for the distortion on these rigs and then when they put it on tape."[26]

O'Brien's interest in such distortions prompts him frequently to mix various means of expression. He likes to smuggle one type of talk into a seemingly inappropriate situation so that we may listen to one way of sounding compete with another. In the first biographical reminiscence, we begin to feel safe having left Finn and his mead and dung-befouled breeches far behind. We begin to get our bearings as we listen to the confidential, "erudite" conversation of the undergraduate when, without warning, echoes of the wide-hammed giant intrude in the description of Kelly:

> I was walking through the Stephen's Green on a summer evening and conducting a conversation with a man called Kelly, then a student, hitherto a member of the farming class, and now a private in the armed forces of the King. He was addicted to unclean expressions in ordinary conversation and spat continually, always fouling the flowerbeds on his way through the Green with a mucous deposit dislodged with a low grunting from the interior of his windpipe. (*AS* 26)

As the alliteration develops ("conducting a conversation," "fouling the flowerbeds," "deposit dislodged"), the passage calls forth the swelling tendency of the Finn descriptions, then seems to resolve and displace itself in one of the narrator's unctuous periphrastic roundabouts. I do not mean to imply that epic alliteration necessarily *produces* the narrator's periphrasis; O'Brien is much too slippery for that. But the two ways of sounding exist in the same sentence, refracting in the manner of oil and water.

We hear the same kind of contention when the uncle is presented through a favorite syntactical arrangement of Finn. When Finn "relates" or "makes," he often encloses an esoteric list with the pronoun "these" and a comprehensive assessment. In reponse to Conan's inquiry about the sweetest music, Finn responds: "I will relate. . . . I like gull-cries and the twittering together of fine cranes. I like the surf-roar at Tralee, the songs of the three sons of Meadhra and the whistle of Mac Lughaidh. These also please me, man shouts at a parting, cuckoo-call in May . . ." (*AS* 16).

During breakfast one morning, the undergraduate asks for five shillings to buy *Die Harzreise*. Over fried haddock, the uncle balks a bit at the price but finally offers two half-crowns. Perhaps in response to such mythic generosity, his nephew temporarily re-makes him through the medium of a Finn-like oration: "The redness of his fingers as he handed out his coins, his occupation with feeding for the nourishment of his body, these were two things that revealed for an instant his equal humanity" (*AS* 44–45).

Perhaps the most recondite, baffling, elliptical section of *At Swim* is the fireside recitation of Mad King Sweeny's treetop adventures. Again, our novelistic inclination is to demand "What has this to do with anything?" Like Furriskey, Shanahan, and Lamont, we are likely to get itchy, anxious to get on to more comprehensive matter. Lamont voices the reader's impulse when he says, "It'll be a good man that'll put a stop to that man's tongue. More of your fancy kiss-my-hand, by God" (*AS* 110). But if we resist our impatience with the unfamiliar, and let our reading be led by hammer, anvil, and stirrup, the arcane prose and poetry prove strangely enjoyable.

Buile Suibhne (The Frenzy of Sweeny) is a middle Irish romance which recounts the high-flying trials and tribulations of one Suibhne Geilt (Sweeny the Madman), king of Dal Araidhe. During the early years of the Catholic church in Ireland, St. Ronan elicits Sweeny's ire by attempting to build a church in Dal Araidhe. Sweeny makes his feelings known by hurling the cleric's psalter into a lake and later inserting his spear into the side of a psalmist, whereupon Ronan metes out a rather severe penance, cursing Sweeny, praying that he "go madly mad-gone/skyward" (*AS* 92). His prayers are answered during the battle of Magh Rath when Sweeny "literally flies, a stark madman, out of the battlefield."[27] From here on, Sweeny is fated to wander throughout Ireland, flying from treetop to thorny treetop, consuming watercress and water, recounting his woes in melodious staves.

One must rely on educated guesswork when trying to determine the source of O'Brien's Sweeny. While Finn MacCool was a pervasive folk and literary tradition, Sweeny, the flying poet of the yew trees, enjoyed no such popularity. In 1913, The Irish Texts Society published the first full translation of *Buile Suibhne* by J. G. O'Keeffe. While O'Brien's account is quite similar to O'Keeffe's, there are significant stylistic differences. Two of the three manuscripts on which O'Keeffe based his translation were available to O'Brien in the Royal Irish Academy.[28] He probably encountered these manuscripts while researching his master's thesis at UCD. Writing to Longmans Green in 1938, he states that he translated *Buile Suibhne* himself. What is most important here is that O'Brien remakes the adventures of Sweeny, conducting the delirium with a pleonastic style which informs the basic procedures of *At Swim*.

By pleonasm, I mean the use of language which emphasizes repetition and redundancy in elaborate excess. For instance, listen to Sweeny's attentive homage to a matriarchal stag:

> Oh mother of this herd,
> thy coat has greyed,
> no stag is following after thee
> without twice twenty points.
>
> Greater-than-the-material-for-a-little-cloak,
> thy head has greyed;
> if I were on each little point
> littler points would there be on every pointed point. (*AS* 113–14)

One must be careful here; the *Buile Suibhne* is by nature pleonastic as a reading of O'Keeffe will indicate. But O'Brien reiterates the romance's inclination to reiteration, elaborating its whorllike tendency to involve itself. This becomes evident in a comparison of O'Keeffe's and O'Brien's rendition of St. Ronan's curse of Sweeny. First O'Keeffe:

> The bell which thou hast wounded
> will send thee among branches,
> so that thou shalt be one with the birds—
> the bell of saints before saints.
>
> Even as in an instant went
> the spear shaft on high,
> mayest thou go, O Suibhne
> in madness, without respite![29]

Now O'Brien:

> The holy bell that thou hast outraged
> will banish thee to branches,
> it will put thee on a par with fowls—
> the saint-bell of saints with sainty-saints.
>
> Just as it went prestissimo
> the spear-shaft skyward,
> you too, Sweeny, go madly mad-gone
> skyward. (*AS* 92)

Karl Miller exhibits an eye and an ear for the spirit and sparkle of such passages when he says of O'Brien's pleonasm: "His excesses recall, and occasionally imitate, the rhetoric of classical Gaelic poetry, the grace notes of bagpipe music, the convolutions and circularities of the illuminated manuscript, of the brooch, of the Celtic cross."[30] The pleonasm of the Sweeny staves looks forward as well as backward, perhaps prompting—but at least participating in—the repetitions and excesses of the last third of the novel.

As a text which spotlights the volatile activity of writing rather than any static, finished product, At Swim discontinually repeats and revises itself. O'Brien's novel demands that readers carefully listen for echoes and repetitions; distorting reverberations emanate the energy of imaginative remaking. As characters mutiny against author, and son against his father, the Buile Suibhne style modulates into Orlick's scriptural torture of Trellis. St. Moling, who assists Sweeny at the end of his life, becomes the St. Ronan figure, disturbing Trellis's sleep and precipitating his torment. In Finn's rendition, St. Ronan angered Sweeny because he "was out in the matin-hours taping out the wall-steads of a new sun-bright church and ringing his bell in the morning" (AS 90). Much later, in Orlick's composition, this description is appropriated and accommodated to suit the mangling of Trellis who is awakened by "a saint in his garden taping out the wallsteads of a new sun-bright church, with a distinguished concourse of clerics and acolytes along with him, discoursing and ringing shrill iron bells and reciting elegant latin" (AS 246). Like Sweeny, Trellis offends the saint by displaying contempt for his holy text and physically attacking the clergy. While Sweeny throws St. Ronan's psalter into a lake and reddens his spear in one of his psalmists, Trellis tears St. Moling's breviary into tatters and hammers one of his acolytes with a stone (AS 90–91 and 246). Their penances also evidence affinities; Trellis's protracted tortures include a Sweenyish insomnia-aggravating roost:

[Finn's Sweeny:]
In that glen it was hard for Sweeny to endure the pain of his bed there on the top of a tall ivy-grown hawthorn in the glen, every twist that he would turn sending showers of hawy thorns into his flesh, tearing and rending and piercing him and pricking his blood-red skin. (AS 94)

[Orlick's Trellis:]
That night they [the Pooka and Trellis] rested at the tree of Cluain Eo, Trellis at his birds'-roost on a thin branch surrounded by tufts of piercing thorns and tangles of bitter spiky brambles. (AS 265)

One must be cautious, however, about aligning such parallels too rigidly; *At Swim* resists the critical effort to fix significance. Just as soon as we think we've got something to hold onto, the handle dissolves and reforms itself beyond our grasp. As J. C. C. Mays says, "The counterpoint method is such that any connection between the parts of the book frustrates another at the same time that it establishes itself."[31]

Just as the lacerating decomposition of Trellis recalls the puncturing of Sweeny, the dialogues between the Pooka and Trellis often echo the Pooka/Good Fairy colloquies which attempt to corral absurdities within "rational," debating procedures:

> Good morning to you, Sir, said the Pooka with melodious intonation. No doubt you have awakened to divert yourself with the refreshment of the dawn.
>
> Trellis composed his pimples the way they would tell of the greatness of the surprise that was in his mind.
>
> Your visit to my house this morning, he said, that surprises me. A bull may sometimes be a cow, a jackdaw may discourse, cocks have established from time to time the hypothesis that the egg is impeculiar to the she-bird, but a servant is at all times a servant notwithstanding. I do not recall that I desired you for a guest at an hour when I am accustomed to be unconscious in the shadow of my sleep. Perchance you bring a firkin of sweet ointment compounded for the relief of boils?
>
> I do not, rejoined the Pooka.
>
> Then a potion, herbal and decanted from the juice of roots, unsurpassed for the extirpation of personal lice?
>
> Doubts as to the sex of cattle, observed the Pooka . . . arise only when the animal is early in its youth. . . . Jackdaws who discourse . . . may betray an indication of the nature of their talent by inadvertently furnishing the same answer to all questions. . . . If a cock may secrete eggs from his interior, equally a hen can crow at four-thirty of a morning. (*AS* 249)

And, as the Pooka replaces St. Moling who superseded St. Ronan, Trellis first assumes the voice of the Good Fairy then breaks into the idiom of Shorty Andrews: "Keep away, you crump, you, he roared. Oh, by God, I'll kick your guts around the room if you don't keep your hands off me!" (*AS* 252).

At the same time, the interruptions of Orlick's text by Furriskey, Shanahan, and Lamont echo their frequent rupturing of Finn MacCool's recital of the staves of Sweeny. Their suggestions for harrowing Trellis also correspond with the hilarious tea table conversation at Mrs. Furriskey's (née Peggy) which canvasses the various agonies of boils, split kneecaps, partial paralysis, and "our old friend pee-eye-ell-ee-ess" (*AS* 229). If one has happened to miss the point that self-parody underlies the myriad of repetitions, I suggest comparing all this hopping from tree to tree to policeman Craddock's legendary leap of *"twenty-four feet six"* which attests to the rationale that "go where you like in the wide world, you will always find that the Irishman is looked up to for his jumping" (*AS* 122).

Locating correspondences in the novel can become a critical parlor game which amuses at first, but ultimately frustrates as it seems to perpetuate its activity by dissolving one structure in order to shape another. This is why I object to the frequency with which critics attempt to put a lid on the novel by "discovering" its counterpoint structure. J. C. C. Mays uses the term acknowledging its makeshift status, but APRoberts claims:

> The apparent chaos of O'Brien's novel, where characters have taken over to an unprecedented extent, is anything but chaos. The parts stand in beautiful and complicated and meaningful relationship to each other and to the whole. "The fugal and contrapuntal character of Bach's work, said the Pooka, that is a delight," and O'Brien delights us in this way, most particularly with what could be called his Great Fugue, the description of the journey to Orlick's birthplace.[32]

Fortunately, the novel is never that neat. To be sure, O'Brien encourages such statements by lacing *At Swim* with musical references. But he is offering the reader one more false bottom; any correlation between the text and harmonic structure is as tentative as it is transient. According to the *Harvard Brief Dictionary of Music*, the fugue is based on a theme, a tonal center, to which "all the devices of imitative counterpoint, such as inversion, stretto, augmentation, diminution, canon," etc. refer.[33] However, *At Swim-Two-Birds* is an eccentric novel devoid of any tonal center. It sometimes seems like a fugue in its display of imaginative invention, but its structure is more protean because words are more unstable than musical notes. In all of its structures, *At Swim* stresses the shifty, shifting propensities of language; as the epigraph of the novel reminds us (in Greek of course), "all things fleet and yield each other place."[34]

The evanescent quality of the text is due, in part to the diverse excesses in which O'Brien indulges. One of the most frantic scenes in the novel is the one APRoberts finds so patterned—the pilgrimage of assorted players to the nativity of Orlick. Before examining how the scene achieves form, I want to call attention to the way a most peculiar sentence seems to build itself.

Near the end of their journey, the Pooka MacPhellimey, Good Fairy, Slug Willard, Shorty Andrews, and Jem Casey encounter Sweeny "the thin-groined" who has literally fallen into their midst. The motley crew encourages the cress-eater to accompany them:

> And getting around the invalid in a jabbering ring, they rubbed him and cajoled and coaxed, and plied him with honey-talk and long sweet-lilted sentences full of fine words, and promised him metheglin and mugs of viscous tar-black mead thickened with white yeast and the spoils from hives of mountain-bees, and corn-coarse nourishing farls of wheaten bread dipped in musk-scented liquors and sodden with Belgian sherry, an orchard and a swarm of furry honey-glutted bees and a bin of sun-bronzed grain from the granaries of the Orient in every drop as it dripped at the lifting of the hand to the mouth, and inky quids of strong-smoked tabacca with cherrywood pipes, hubble-bubbles, duidins, meerschaums, clays, hickory hookahs and steel-stemmed pipes with enamel bowls, the lot of them laid side by side in a cradle of lustrous blue plush, a huge pipe-case and pipe-rack ingeniously combined and circumscribed with a durable quality of black imitation leather over a framework of stout cedarwood dovetailed and intricately worked and made to last, the whole being handsomely finished and untouched by hand and packed in good-quality transparent cellophane, a present calculated to warm the cockles of the heart of any smoker. (*AS* 183–84)

As one might guess, such a sentence is appreciated best when read aloud. In its extravagance, this passage says a lot about the way O'Brien writes; he spends himself in excess, willing to risk losing authorial control for the pleasures of abandoning himself to the thrusts of divergent modes of expression. He starts the ball rolling, then half steers, half hangs on as stylistic forms assume a motion and direction of their own, landing him in an unplanned-for environment.

This two-hundred-and-eleven-word sentence exaggerates a propensity for building itself vertically as well as horizontally. As the reader (or preferably speaker) makes her way through linearly, she is held up by a variety of verbs: "rubbed," "cajoled," "coaxed," "plied," and "promised," and then by a sequence of presents promised: "metheglin," "mugs," "farls," "orchard," "swarm," "bin," "quids," "pipes," etc. Many of the items in these synchronic detours seem determined to expand themselves in protracted prepositional phrases. It seems as if the sentence were responding to an anxiety about saying one thing by not saying another. By the time one arrives at the pipe-case and pipe-rack, the structure returns to the syntactical pattern with which it began and, as Furriskey is wont to say, "we're off again."

More urgent, however, is the way an identifiable aural pattern emerges, begins to exert its influence on the sentence, then finally gives way. In the introductory phrase, we encounter a rather nondescript voice, difficult to name, perhaps the voice of a novelistic third person narrator trying to efface himself. But before we have finished the list of verbs, we hear the Finn MacCool style taking shape in the alliteration and hyphenated adjectival constructions. In the list of objects promised, the Finn canon is in full force; we recognize the familiar drone and the unfamiliar vocabulary, as well as the bardic incremental penchant. (The hocus-pocus comes from inhaling through "hubble-bubbles" and "hickory hookahs.") But this verbal deluge takes its toll. Finn's voice seems to exhaust itself, giving way to, perhaps in some indirect way establishing a current for, the commercial jargon of modern manufacturing. The pipes will be covered in "black imitation leather . . . handsomely finished and untouched by hand and packed in good-quality transparent cellophane." It's as if we've already traveled over a thousand years in a single sentence, vaulting from an ancient agrarian harvest to a present day production line. Robert Frost would ask of such extravagance, "Can you go with it?"[35]

When I said earlier that the "happy mission" to the Red Swan Hotel is a most frantic scene, I was referring to the way a medley of voices accumulates, competes, arranges, and rearranges itself at a tempo which dazzles as it discomposes us. The journey commences with the annoying Good Fairy commanding, "keep to the left," and arguing with the urbane Pooka about the quality of his suit: "the best cloth that could be had . . . cost me five and sixpence a yard" (AS 160–61). As they proceed, the Pooka and the Good Fairy soon meet a couple of cowboys out looking for a lost steer: the courteous Slug Willard, "adroitly donning his wet hat the way he could raise it for politeness," and the pugnacious Shorty Andrews, "your porridge" (AS 163–64). As soon as Jem Casey falls in with the lot and treats them to a blue-collar doggerel, "The Gift of God is a Workin' Man," they discover something up a tree. By now we are listening to an aural kaleidoscope turning through polychromatic permutations of: whether the Good Fairy is a ferret or can fly; what Jem Casey was doing in the bushes; the nature of the Pooka's wife; if Shorty should shoot the thing in the tree that hasn't got trousers on; and how the word "kangaroo" is contained in the word "marsupial" (*AS* 167–77). As Sweeny falls, "percolated through the sieve of a sharp yew," he adds his voice in melodious lays. This prompts another round of cacaphonous jabber, as they wonder: whether the newcomer is "one of the Sweenies of Rathangan" or "the Sweenies of Swanlibar"; whether he be drunk or has a fever, "has anybody got a thermometer till we take his pulse?"; and whether the best prescription is a bullet to "put him out of his pain," "a glass of gin and a bottle of stone beer," or "damp sponges of lichen and green moss" (*AS* 178–82).

The discordant voices play off one another, convening and dispersing at a disconcerting pace which threatens to get out of hand. The zaniness here approaches that of the Marx Brothers in the final scene of *Monkey Business* where the violence in the barn is refracted by Groucho's play-by-play report and Harpo's wheel-of-fortune game. Juggling a tail, a pair of wings, a lasso, a sixgun, a spade, and a bloody thorn, O'Brien creates fantastic if absurd forms in the air while astounding himself, and us, with his dexterity. There is, to borrow his own phrase, "a surprising kinesis of many incalculable influences" (*AS* 252).

Through all such performances, O'Brien advertently and ambitiously tests the vulnerability of authoring. In many of the traditions to which he refers, including for the most part the realistic novel, the potency of language usually stands unquestioned. In the bardic mode of Finn MacCool, the verbal magic of phonetic patterning generates marvelous exploits. *Buile Suibhne* also celebrates the ability of words to beget experience; it is, after all, St. Ronan's curse (elicited by violence to a text) which sends Sweeny flying. The persecution of Trellis is similarly powered by words; the author is almost physically deconstructed by his characters inscribing characters in a notebook. Orlick explains: "I have conceived some extremely recondite pains for Mr. Trellis. I will pierce him with a pluperfect" (*AS* 242). And the ideal of "the word made flesh" is realized as John Furriskey achieves a spontaneous, fully formed existence through the agency of aestho-autogamy. Thanks to the pioneering of Mr. Tracy and the wonders of modern science, the operations of sperm and egg are replaced by those of pen and paper. In all of these instances, one senses, on the part of O'Brien, an attitude of wistful wish fulfillment; he seems to long for the possibilities afforded by myth when one might create experience simply by speaking or writing. At the same time, however, O'Brien parodies the notion of fecund language as well as the supposed genealogical relationship between author and text:

> It is noteworthy that Mr. Tracy [the "original author" of aestho-auto-gamy] succeeded, after six disconcerting miscarriages, in having his own wife delivered of a middle-aged Spaniard who lived for only six weeks. A man who carried jealousy to the point of farce, the novelist insisted that his wife and the new arrival should occupy separate beds and use the bathroom at divergent times. Some amusement was elicted in literary circles by the predicament of a woman who was delivered of a son old enough to be her father. (*AS* 56–57)

The worries of Mr. Tracy are those of Mr. O'Brien. *At Swim* explores the extent to which an author's "progeny," a word or any structure made with words, might assume and exercise an authority of its own. Mutiny, as a focal concern in the novel, is evident from the opening autograph jottings of *MS1*. On the first page of the manuscript, O'Brien penned "a little bastard" four times, with one entry centered and underlined (*MS1* 1). Leaf four presents an autograph list of "Personnel" with a key addition squeezed in: "Characters in order of their disappearance" (*MS1* 4). Here, the "poor bastard" is identified as "Little Orlick" who perpetrates the ultimate revolt, attempting to write his author/father out of existence. The rebellion of Trellis's characters may be taken as a metaphor for the seditious propensity of discourse, its proclivity for running away from its author and propelling, however temporarily, structures of its own. The complications, confusions, as well as comedy of *At Swim* issue from O'Brien's own "inverted sow neurosis wherein the farrow eat their dam" (*AS* 314–15).

While *At Swim* is consciously written against the measure of moments, it also, just as willfully, exposes the inability of any means of shaping to sustain itself through a passage of time. In the protracted, peculiar sentence previously analyzed, in which the troop attempts to revive Sweeny with "honey-talk . . . full of fine words," we hear a pseudonovelistic narrative voice give way to the bardic style of Finn MacCool (which temporarily takes charge, effecting a swollen, labyrinthine shape), then finally collapse into incongruous mercantile jargon concerning "a durable quality of black imitation leather . . . handsomely finished and untouched by hand and packed in good-quality transparent cellophane . . ." (*AS* 184).

On a larger level, this procedure illustrates the basic disposition of the novel. During its fragmenting process, one means of expression displaces another, exhausts its formative vigor, and is itself superseded by an alternative style. Each manner of making confirms its inherent shaping potency yet, given time, reveals its tenuous inability to finish, to complete itself. The novel is not so much a parody of any particular discourse as it is a parody of the undergraduate's, Finn's, the press's, Sweeny's, Orlick's, and O'Brien's own efforts to achieve lasting shape with words. A parallel charge informs Beckett's *Murphy* (published in 1938 while *At Swim* was being rejected by various publishers). In response to Murphy's ways with words, Celia muses:

> She felt, as she felt so often with Murphy, spattered with words that went dead as soon as they sounded; each word obliterated, before it had time to make sense, by the word that came next; so that in the end she did not know what had been said. It was like difficult music heard for the first time.[36]

It is important to keep in mind, however, just how playfully O'Brien handles these compelling matters. While the breakdown of discursive strategies has been made an urgent concern of academic reading, it is often the occasion for sport in *At Swim*. The scene, previously discussed, in which Furriskey, Shanahan, and Lamont supplement Orlick's text and then deny their additions, is teeming with comic paradoxes. For me, the most intriguing is the suggestion that an author can erase himself and all traces of his presence *while he writes*. O'Brien compulsively complicates the activity of writing, seeming simultaneously to affirm and deny the self as it seeks to achieve presence on paper. He does not dwell on these propositions, forcing them into "issues," but, invariably, he demonstrates his awareness that the attempt to impart form, to give shape, is risky business. Language shows signs of running away with itself; characters turn on their author; all discourse dissolves unable to endure duration.

Yet O'Brien seems to consider the precariousness of authorship as more an enabling condition than a restraint, acting as if he derives some strange innovative energy from discharging language. Although never quite sure to what degree he creates, participates in, or observes discursive fracturing, he inevitably seizes the occasion as an opportunity to begin again, to "re-begin," to begin over.

Next to "spare-time," the narrator's favorite word to describe his literary activities is "recreative," an apt adjective for O'Brien's fictions. They are "recreative" in the sense that they are refreshing, diverting activities, play, and they are "re-creative" in that they create anew. Reading *At Swim,* we are asked to conceive of the novel as palimpsest, as a text written upon other texts which are still partially visible, having been imperfectly erased. Beginning means rewriting but, more significantly, it means writing over what has been written before.

It is not my purpose here to catalogue all the rewriting of the novel, that is a job better left to makers of conspecti, but a few examples should help us recall the prominence of the activity. Obviously, the "three separate openings" which commence the novel appear later in modified forms and new contexts. The person of Trellis is extensively and repeatedly revised first by the narrator and Brinsley, then later by Orlick, Furriskey, Shanahan, and Lamont; and, of course, Mad Sweeny is rewritten from Finn's renditions to Orlick's plagiaristic appropriation. One would think that in listening to Shanahan's advice for Orlick, we were overhearing O'Brien talking to himself: "Certainly you can begin again, said Shanahan, there's no harm done, man. I've been longer in this world and I can tell you this: *There's nothing to be ashamed of in a false start.* We can but try. Eh, boys? We can but try" (*AS* 243 [O'Brien's italics]).

Examining the inadequacies of language a minute ago, I considered styles emerging and exhausting themselves sequentially, contending with tangentially prior and subsequent forms. I want now to reconsider the impotence of writing, given the way human memory competes with time. In emphasizing the novel as palimpsest, O'Brien asks that we recall particular styles and events that are "like" the one we are presently reading, consciously "stacking" them, superimposing one upon others. By looking and listening through the text immediately before our eyes to and through other like texts which have been displaced by duration, we discover the most interesting and creative distortions. Lillian Hellman describes the effect I am talking about when she defines "pentimento":

Old paint on canvas, as it ages, sometimes becomes transparent. When that happens it is possible, in some pictures, to see the original lines: a tree will show through a woman's dress, a child makes way for a dog, a large boat is no longer on an open sea. That is called pentimento because the painter "repented," changed his mind. Perhaps it would be as well to say that the old conception, replaced by a later choice, is a way of seeing and then seeing again.[37]

The moments of keenest exhilaration and enthusiasm are those in which a structure shaped by a previous literature or a structure previously shaped by O'Brien, shows through the passage we are reading, signifying, however fleetingly, the tenacious resistance of writing to eradication.

Viewing the novel as palimpsest, we are also reminded of the disparity between words and things, and that language necessarily refers to itself. The activity of fiction making is parodied but so is the widely held belief that literature is in some way secondary to, or a substitute for, a true reality taking place beyond the reach of the page. Since each means of expression refers to another, O'Brien gives the lie to the truth of newspapers, encyclopedias, and watches. They are, more excitingly than merely, other fictions, alternative ways of arranging what can be known. The experience of reading *At Swim-Two-Birds* is not unlike watching the rendition of a comic stripper's routine. Taking one's time, the performer peels a layer of clothing, tantalizing the audience's expectations. Yet each article divested exposes beneath it another smaller, more stylish costume. The process repeats itself over and over, never revealing "the goods," but instead accentuating the spectacle as performance. In like manner, O'Brien teasingly exposes fictions beneath fictions, highlighting that the goods are themselves fictitious.[38]

As we make our way through the novel, we are witness to someone having a good time having his way with words, extending himself, penetrating discourses. Almost like the poor German who closes the book, O'Brien risks taking razor to jugular as he writes, realizing that the activity may be cutting his own throat, but nevertheless grinning as he scribbles "good-bye, good-bye, good-bye" (*AS* 316).

4

The Third Policeman: "Re-Inscribing" the Self

Life's but a walking shadow, a poor player,
That struts and frets his hour upon the stage
And then is heard no more. It is a tale
Told by an idiot, full of sound and fury,
Signifying nothing.

—*Macbeth*, V, v, 24–28.

If you ever enjoy the accident of looking at a television screen through the medium of an electric fan, you might be startled and intrigued to discover an empirical contradiction. Although turning very rapidly, the blades of the fan will be clearly visible and will appear to be stationary. The effect is a stroboscopic illusion produced by the interaction of the television's pulsating picture with the fan's compatible speed of revolution. The television picture we perceive as continuous is actually composed of electronic beams which flash on and off sixty times every second. We see this as a steady light because our physical and cognitive capabilities can not keep up with the rapidity of the pulsations. If a fan turning at the right speed is placed between the eye and the screen, however, television's operational characteristics reveal themselves indirectly. A fan turning at sixty revolutions per second, or a simple multiple of that speed, correlates with the frequency of the electronic beams, and the blades of the fan seem to stand still. The eye and the brain are again mistaken—but in a novel way. It is an instance when the refutation of the normal can call into question our means of knowing.[1]

This experience corresponds with the protagonist's predicament in *The Third Policeman*. He has learned to rely on modes of perception, thought, and speech which ostensibly account for and exert control over daily phenomena. Just when "normal" cognitive prerogatives seem assured, however, he finds a metaphoric fan thrust in his way, bringing both itself and him to a standstill. While circular in structure, the novel centers on the narrator's provocative reevaluation of fields of knowledge and his sense of self. This first-person narrative of an absent character may be seen as the attempt to defer death, to avoid anonymity, to mediate an existence in the verification of voice.

The Third Policeman begins by establishing a world with which we think we are familiar. Its environment resembles the one we participate in daily where time, chemical reactions, and the laws of motion conform to our notion of normal reality. In a conventional and deliberately mundane manner, we meet our protagonist, the anonymous narrator around whom all events reportedly revolve. He tells us the history of his birth, schooling, postgraduate ambitions—the experiences which have shaped his existence up until now. All is related in the tried-and-true format for a "life," with sequential, progressive arrangements resulting in the product at hand.

The entire first chapter (and a page or two of the second) is a setup designed to fix a traditional territory from which the beat of Policeman Pluck will sharply diverge. The standard—against which subsequent deviances can be measured—is a reasonable world of latitude and longitude, girders and panels, and commutative, developmental operations. Language and environment seem to correspond comfortably; words supposedly name and stably place the things to which they refer. Here, the narrator learns to "situate" himself as he masters the accepted verbal stock and repertoire of arrangements which account for his existence.

From the outset, we hear a voice self-consciously concerned with accommodating experience to the characteristic forms of narrative. The novel opens:

> Not everybody knows how I killed old Phillip Mathers, smashing his jaw in with my spade; but first it is better to speak of my friendship with John Divney because it was he who first knocked old Mathers down by giving him a great blow in the neck with a special bicycle pump which he manufactured himself out of a hollow iron bar. (*TP* 7)

In the midst of a casual reference to a murder, fraught with comically extravagant details, we hear a colloquial voice attempting to interrupt the linear process of his speech and reorder his narrative. We must "first" hear of John Divney because he "first" started things with a bicycle pump which originated as a metal bar. The voice is trying to replace what comes after the first line in a position of priority to demonstrate how one circumstance or event begets another. Put simply, he wants to stabilize his experi-

ence by shaping the events of his life according to the logic of
cause and effect. As in the billiards section of *At Swim-Two-Birds*,
the influence of David Hume is felt strongly. In *A Treatise of Human
Nature*, Hume states:

> Tis evident that all reasonings concerning matter of fact are founded
> on the relation of cause and effect, and that we can never infer the
> existence of one object from another unless they be connected to-
> gether either mediately or immediately. . . . It follows then, that all
> reasonings concerning cause and effect are founded on experience,
> and that all reasonings from experience are founded on the supposi-
> tion that the course of nature will continue uniformly the same.[2]

The methods which the opening of the novel sets up, and the rest
of the novel challenges, are derived from the "reasonings"
through which one infers existence. Experience apparently testifies that words and knowledge are "connected together" through
serial arrangements which correspond with genealogical relationships. Traditionally, narrative derives its authority and power
to reassure from its reinscription of familiar patternings.

The narrator's conscious concern for properly structuring his
tale in causal procedures "naturally" leads to a discussion of his
origin:

> I was born a long time ago. My father was a strong farmer and my
> mother owned a public house. We all lived in the public house but it
> was not a strong house at all and was closed most of the day because
> my father was out at work on the farm and my mother was always in
> the kitchen and for some reason customers never came until it was
> nearly bed-time; and well after it at Christmas-time and on other
> unusual days like that. I never saw my mother outside the kitchen in
> my life and never saw a customer during the day and even at night I
> never saw more than two or three together. But then I was in bed part
> of the time and it is possible that things happened differently with my
> mother and with the customers late at night. (*TP* 7)

Presenting a brief description of his parents, the narrator
adopts a childlike perspective of innocence and insecurity. His
precarious handling of language dramatizes the inability to
"read"—to recognize—the world. Vocabulary and sentence structures are exceedingly simple and obviously imprecise. Monosylla-
bles are the order of the day while most clauses are strung
together with the colloquial "and." The word "strong" is repeated
four times on the first page without any indication that the

speaker can distinguish between a "strong house" and a "strong farmer" who owns the property. His difficulty managing words often results in humorous ambiguities. Smiling at the possibility that "things happened differently with my mother and with the customers late at night," readers think they perceive a salacious suggestion beyond a child's ken. The unintended intimation of the mother's infidelity, however, comically tenders one of the focal concerns of the novel. The problems of identity and authority for a bastard in this world will be aggravatingly compounded in the country of Sergeant Pluck. The question of his patrimony becomes moot, however, as the narrator's attempt to shape his existence in familiar progressions runs into a different sort of snag:

> Then a certain year came about the Christmas-time and when the year was gone my father and mother were gone also. Mick the sheepdog was very tired and sad after my father went and would not do his work with the sheep at all; he too went the next year. I was young and foolish at the time and did not know properly why these people had all left me, where they had gone and why they did not give explanations beforehand. My mother was the first to go and I can remember a fat man with a red face and a black suit telling my father that there was no doubt where she was, that he could be as sure of that as he could of anything else in this vale of tears. But he did not mention where and as I thought the whole thing was very private and that she might be back on Wednesday, I did not ask him where. Later, when my father went, I thought he had gone to fetch her with an outside car but when neither of them came back on the next Wednesday, I felt sorry and disappointed. The man in the black suit was back again. He stayed in the house for two nights and was continually washing his hands in the bedroom and reading books. There were two other men, one a small pale man and one a tall black man in leggings. They had pockets full of pennies and they gave me one every time I asked them questions. I can remember the tall man in the leggings saying to the other man:
>   "The poor misfortunate little bastard."
>   I did not understand this at the time and thought that they were talking about the other man in the black clothes who was always working at the wash-stand in the bedroom. But I understood it all clearly afterwards. (*TP* 8)

The comic confusion centers on a basic discrepancy between experience and the language of experience. As a child, the narrator perceives the absence of his parents yet his know-how with words is inadequate to a "proper" understanding of the event. He misinterpets the grownups voicing their predilection for palliating death in colloquial euphemism. His mother is "gone," but a priest assures his father that "there was no doubt where she was, that he could be as sure of that as he could of anything else in this vale of tears." Literalizing the metaphor of death as a journey, the child logically assumes that his mother should return shortly—perhaps on a Wednesday in an unusual vehicle. As readers, we smile because we think we are beyond being so naive as to mistake the identity of "the poor misfortunate little bastard." We assume (as the narrator does later) that we comprehend the proceedings clearly and "know properly why these people had all left." Our experience and expertise with language consume the anxieties of death in humor. But the novel later makes clear that any such smug security is infinitely foolish and disturbingly dangerous.

With time and more experience, our dubious hero learns to "name" what lies before him. Upon completing an education at a reputable institution, he confides: "I had long-since got to know how I was situated in the world" (*TP* 9). He then "places" himself through social relationships and demonstrates his self-knowledge with a chronological rendition of his schooling, travels, and dedication to de Selby. After acquiring the complete works of the master, along with those of his major and minor commentators, he spends years of academic anemia pedantically arranging their authority in systematic discourse: "I had completed my definitive 'De Selby Index' wherein the views of all known commentators on every aspect of the savant and his work had been collated" (*TP* 14). Somewhere amidst this arduous training, he has picked up a working knowledge of the subtle indirections of language.

While presenting his brief biography, he casually offers indications that he has become more familiar with these artifacts, words. John Divney, who manages the narrator's public house, continually complains of his financial straitjacketing:

> As time went on Divney became more and more despondent about what he called "the bar." He said that he would be satisfied if it paid its way but he doubted seriously if it ever would. . . . He did not think that he could continue to bear the burden of the loss without some assistance. (*TP* 12)

Curiously, Mr. Divney cries poor mouth while contriving to outfit himself regularly with new suits and expensive tiepins. The scholar handles the curate quite deftly: "I said that my father had some old-fashioned way of management which made possible a profit but that the shop should be closed if now continuing to lose money. Divney only said that it was a very serious thing to surrender a licence" (*TP* 12).

The narrator evinces an even more interesting proficiency with language when he explains how he and Divney acquired the reputation of "great friends." Our orphan-scholar confides that he has led a rather solitary existence; his academic endeavors and wooden leg have obliged an indoor lifestyle separate from social commerce: "Then something very unusual happened to change all this and after it had happened, Divney and I never parted company for more than one minute either night or day" (*TP* 12–13). We are then treated to an extensive list of their shared activities; they eat, sleep, and, presumably, make water together. If Divney courts a certain party of a Sunday afternoon, our man makes the company a crowd; if Divney gets the urge for a late night stroll, he is accompanied regardless of the torrential gale outside. Their inseparability continues for three years while the community hails them as the ultimate example of friendship and the "two best Christians in all Ireland" (*TP* 13).

What proves intriguing here is the narrator's meticulous enumeration of effects prior to the revelation of their cause. Apparently the earlier anxiety over elementary linear form has given way to a conscious confidence with building verbal structures. Now, he deliberately defers sequential order through omission; like a skilled stand-up comic, he makes us wait for the punch line: "I must go back several years to explain what happened to bring about this peculiar situation" (*TP* 13–14).

The punch line is, in fact, a death blow to the jaw with a spade. The reader returns for a moment to the situation with which the novel opens, and joins the ranks of the "not everybody" who "knows how I killed old Phillip Mathers." What has happened, of course, is an unresolved crime perpetrated by the narrator and Divney. They rob Mathers together, but Divney hides the money while his accomplice buries the body:

> In the weeks which followed I asked him where the box was a hundred times in a thousand different ways. He never answered in the same way but the answer was always the same. It was in a very safe place. The least said about it the better until things quieted down. Mum was the word. It would be found all in good time. For the purpose of safe-keeping the place it was in was superior to the Bank of England. There was a good time coming. It would be a pity to spoil everything by hastiness or impatience. (*TP* 18)

Our storyteller now knows his way around with words, however, and will not mistake Divney's phrases the way he did the tall man's as a child. The names may be changed to protect the culprit but the various configurations all share a single reference:

> And that is why John Divney and I became inseparable friends and why I never allowed him to leave my sight for three years. Having robbed me in my own public house (having even robbed my customers) and having ruined my farm, I knew he was sufficiently dishonest to steal my share of Mathers' money and make off with the box if given the opportunity. (*TP* 18)

The companions then are at the mercy of dishonor among thieves.

I suspect that O'Brien is taking off from a similar situation in Charles Maturin's *Melmoth the Wanderer*. In order to escape the tortures of the Spanish Inquisition, Moncada joins forces with an avowed murderer who has the key to a subterranean passage. If they make good their escape, each will know the other's compromising secret. Ironically, the liberty they desire will be severely restricted by the necessity of watching each other at all times. Once inside the vault, the murderer tells Moncada:

> Our situation has happened to unite very opposite characters in the same adventure, but it is a union inevitable and inseparable. Your destiny is now bound to mine by a tie which no human force can break—we part no more forever. The secret that each of us is in possession of must be watched by the other. . . . We must pass life in watching every breath the other draws, every glance the other gives. . . . We may hate each other—worst of all we may be weary of each other . . . but separate we must never.[3]

While the events in the two novels are similar, the authors cultivate somewhat different responses. Maturin draws the reader in, prompting him to partake of gothic psychological terror; O'Brien holds us back, however, recommending a perspective of more distance. Throughout *The Third Policeman*, he colors the anxieties of death with comedy, although the high humor of the opening turns black and more terrifying as the novel progresses. We are never allowed to take Mathers' murder seriously. Like the death of the parents, it is delivered and accepted with a smile:

> Divney went forward at once and pointing back along the road said:
>   "Would that be your parcel on the road?"

The old man turned his head to look and received a blow in the back of the neck from Divney's pump which knocked him clean off his feet and probably smashed his neck-bone. As he collapsed full-length in the mud he did not cry out. Instead I heard him say something softly in a conversational tone—something like "I do not care for celery" or "I left my glasses in the scullery." Then he lay very still. (*TP* 16)

What in a realistic novel might be a gruesome scene is here a comic vehicle for verbal play. The nonsense of "celery" and "scullery" diverts us from any serious contemplation of the characters' sin. Some critics, however, consider the fifth commandment written in stone and insist on a parochial point of view. Clissmann refers to the domain of Policeman Pluck as "a hell earned for the crime" and claims that the narrator is sent there "to punish him for committing a crime."[4] I doubt that O'Brien is even mildly interested in moral themes of crime and punishment. Let us not forget that in *At Swim-Two-Birds*, Dermot Trellis is unmercifully lampooned for constructing a novel "on sin and the wages attaching thereto" (*AS* 47). The first chapter of *The Third Policeman* essentially operates as a norm against which the rest of the novel can push. We watch the narrator develop a naive confidence in language only to have the rug pulled out from under him. He tumbles into a district where the stabilizing procedures of language which he has learned to trust are abruptly invalidated. He dies, not in retribution for his sins, but to allow the subsequent adventures in verbal invention which wonderfully complicate notions of presence.

In *The Wizard of Oz*, when Dorothy's farmhouse descends out of the whirlwind, she looks around noticing strange flowers, diminutive people, and the gleaming witch Glinda. She then confides to her terrier Toto, "I have a feeling we're not in Kansas anymore." O'Brien would have appreciated such an understatement as an apt analogue for the narrator's misgivings when he finds himself on the other side of "reality."[5] John Divney has sent his partner to retrieve the moneybox hidden under a floorboard in Mathers's house. Needless to say, the cache is booby-trapped, effectively decomposing the storyteller long before his text is fully realized. The fun and the resources of the novel, however, depend upon the deferment of this knowledge. After "death," the narrator encounters phenomena which at first appear consistent with the world previously established, but he gradually discovers himself in a realm of "unreasonable jumps" and "ungovernable inexactitudes" where none of the relied upon rules of time, physics, or physicality hold up in the wash (*TP* 152). The ensuing rigamarole is produced by a perplexing tension between the narrator's style—the verbal patternings and rhythms he has come to trust—and a novel environment orchestrated in a bewildering tempo. This conflict becomes captivating as it urges him to question how his existence is caught up in the ability to name and be named.

The first indication of the conundrums which follow occurs when our man arrives at Mathers's house and inexplicably decides to enter through a window rather than the door:

> Standing on a derelict flower-bed, I tried to push up the sash of the first window on the left. It yielded to my strength raspingly and stubbornly. I clambered through the opening and found myself, not at once in a room, but crawling along the deepest window-ledge I have ever seen. When I reached the floor and jumped noisily down upon it, the open window seemed far away and much too small to have admitted me. (*TP* 22)

Although this "wondrous strange" passage is only touched on, it promises peculiar proceedings in the manner of Alice's rabbithole to Wonderland; the narrator's ominous misgivings will soon be compounded. Following Divney's instructions, he locates the designated hiding place, lifts the loose floorboard, and grasps the handle of the cashbox. Then, "something happened." This impenetrable "something" is left unnamed and for a long time unnamable. The attempt to convey the effects of some unspecified cause, however, forces the narrator to notice a perturbing impotence in his language:

> I cannot hope to describe what it was but it had frightened me very much long before I had understood it even slightly. It was some change which came upon me or upon the room, indescribably subtle, yet momentous, ineffable. It was as if the daylight had changed with unnatural suddenness, as if the temperature of the evening had altered greatly in an instant or as if the air had become twice as rare or twice as dense as it had been in the winking of an eye; perhaps all of these and other things happened together for all my senses were bewildered all at once and could give me no explanation. (*TP* 23)

He attempts to settle himself and to ease the anxiety of bewilderment by verbally placing the experience within the structures of language which previously presumed control. Reverting to the security of chronological order, he carefully arranges his fright "long before" the onset of even slight understanding. But such a structure quickly collapses when he has to admit "perhaps all of these and other things happened together." The confusion of "or" 's—did the change come to him or to the room? did the air become more rare or more dense?—and the concession of "perhaps" indicate his inability to manage the experience with words. His sensations are noticeably at odds with his means of explanation.

The scene which follows is ludicrous and logically impossible, sounding the keynote of absurdity which reverberates throughout the rest of the novel. Old Phillip Mathers, skull crushed with a bicycle pump, body hacked to pieces, buried in a bog for three years, sits silently in a rocking chair, pouring himself tea. Confronted with a bizarre environment of unnatural phenomena, the narrator discovers that "known words" are invalid, inoperative, and futile. His problems in language seem similar to those of Charlie Marlow in *Heart of Darkness* who says to the crew of the *Nellie:*

> It seems to me I am trying to tell you a dream—making a vain attempt, because no relation of a dream can convey the dream-sensation, that commingling of absurdity, surprise, and bewilderment in a tremor of struggling revolt, that notion of being captured by the incredible which is of the very essence of dreams.[6]

Marlow voices the disturbing discrepancy we have all felt between the sensations of a dream and the "re-presentation" of those sensations with words. The telling of the dream seems to falsify or fictionalize it; the sensations themselves, experienced as rationally incoherent, are accommodated to verbal procedures governed by reasonable systems of arrangement. The words "absurd" and "struggling revolt" testify to the inability to locate precisely how the representation misses the mark. Unable to pinpoint the inadequacies, one feels "captured," somehow contained by deficient, perverting means of telling. Addressing this tension between the dream experience and its verbal representation, Freud says: "Elements in this complicated whole which are in fact simultaneous can only be represented successively in my description of them, while, in putting forward each point, I must avoid appearing to anticipate the grounds on which it is based."[7] The presence of a dream is first modified when we become aware of it; a further alteration occurs in the telling; and another distortion accompanies analysis of it. Each stage subtly reshapes; each verbal arrangement necessarily warps the dream. The act of untangling and organizing creates a "version" grounded in and limited by inherent, often undiagnosed rules of formation.

The experiences of the narrator in *The Third Policeman* correspond with dream sensations in the way they resist awareness, telling, or analysis. He is imprisoned not so much by Pluck's jail cell as by the reasonable mental procedures which he has learned to depend on as his means of knowledge. His mistake is in trying to make sense of this incredible environment using logical operations appropriate for the credible world he has just left.

Tendering his first impressions of the dead, rocking Mathers, he speaks hesitantly yet revealingly:

> I remember that I noticed several things in a cold mechanical way as if I was sitting there with no worry save to note everything I saw. His face was terrifying but his eyes . . . were horrible. Looking at them I got the feeling that they were not genuine eyes at all but mechanical dummies animated by electricity or the like, with a tiny pinhole in the centre of the "pupil" through which the real eye gazed out secretively and with great coldness. Such a conception, possibly with no foundation at all in fact, disturbed me agonisingly and gave rise in my mind to interminable speculations as to the colour and quality of the real eye and as to whether, indeed, it was real at all or merely another dummy with its pinhole on the same plane as the first one so that the real eye, possibly behind thousands of these absurd disguises, gazed out through a barrel of serried peep-holes. (*TP* 24–25)

Given the circumstances, such paranoia would be understandable; I am more interested, however, in examining the mechanized mental procedures which spawn such a conception. The word "mechanical" dominates the talk here (appearing five times within a few pages), revealing the narrator's characteristic means of establishing order. He is steeply inclined to think in terms of chronological sequence, serried planes, Riemann integral, calibration, and compilation. His language—grounded in mathematics and physics—has geared him for causal, derivative processes which seek to stabilize by measuring and directing forces encountered. These strategies are disabled by the substantative "places" in which he finds himself. The physical structures of the novel act as spatial metaphors for the verbal passages through which he tries to negotiate a self.

Approaching Policeman Pluck's barracks, the narrator notices that the edifice appears flat, like a Hollywood prop, devoid of depth, as if "one of the customary dimensions was missing, leaving no meaning in the remainder" (*TP* 53). The closer he gets, the more it seems to change its appearance, "building" a third dimension, seeming "to reconcile itself with the shape of an ordinary house" (*TP* 53). At this point, his perspective is still dominated by ordinary order. Only when the structure conforms to his sense of what's "sensible," can he pretend to comprehend it.

Later in the novel, the narrator's normal means of understanding is invalidated further by a strange phenomenon in Mathers's house. Attracted to a lighted window on the second story, the narrator enters, climbs the stairs, and proceeds down the hall, systematically opening doors, searching for the source of the light. As each room reveals only dark emptiness, he puzzles over an apparent empirical impossibility. His confusion is compounded when he walks back down and outside, and looks up to find the light still streaming from the same window. Quickly mounting the stairs again, he recommences a determined investigation with methodical ratiocination:

> I then walked into the room which seemed most in the centre of the house and made my way over to the window in the dark. . . . What I saw from the window startled me painfully. The light was streaming from the window of the room next door on my right hand side . . . playing on the dark green leaves of a tree that stood nearby. (*TP* 177)[8]

Thinking that he has pinpointed the source of illumination, he keeps his gaze fixed on the lighted leaves and slowly backs out of the room. Reaching the hallway, he bounds into the room on his right, only to discover it black and deserted:

> I moved to the window and looked out. The yellow light was still lying on the air and shining on the same tree-leaves but now it was streaming from the window of the room I had just left. I felt I was standing within three yards of something unspeakably inhuman. . . .
> I stopped thinking, closing my mind up with a snap as if it were a box or a book. (*TP* 177–78)

The phenomenon remains "unspeakable" so long as it is approached through the corridors of logic. His source of understanding, located in language, proves as elusive as the light itself. The mystery is incomprehensibly "explained" when Policeman Fox leads him through a wonderland entrance in the side of the building, up a set of "unbelievable" stairs, to his brightly lit "very surprising apartment" (*TP* 182). This room, of most unusual dimensions, seems to exist in an architectural twilight zone.

Noticing a window, the narrator walks over and peers out: "The lamplight was shining dimly on the foliage of the same tree and I knew that I was standing, not in Mathers' house, *but inside the walls of it*" (*TP* 182 [O'Brien's italics]). I intend to return to this crazy outpost of the "Third Policeman" a bit later, but now I would like to consider how these out of whack structures signify.

Thinking through the processes of creative composition, James Merrill voices an interesting correspondence between arrangements in dwellings and arrangements in language: "Interior spaces, the shapes and correlation of rooms in a house, have always appealed to me. . . . This fondness for given arrangements might explain how instinctively I took to quatrains, octaves, and sestets when I began to write poems. 'Stanza' is after all the Italian word for 'room.' "9 Policeman Pluck's barracks and Fox's outpost ambivalently alarm and invite as they contend with the familiar models which correspond with—and are known through—procedures of reason. The "stanzas" of their world, constructed with skewed lines and oblique angles, tilt at the formations we are used to. Sometime between preschool and puberty, children learn to make sense of the structures in which they spend time. A young girl begins to recognize, for instance, the corner of her bedroom where the drainpipe gurgles as "the same" but above the corner of the dining room which sounds similarly during rainstorms. With practice, she develops the ability to abstractly place contained spaces, connecting them with corridors, walls, stairs, and ceilings. One day, from out on the lawn, she discovers that she can mentally cross-section her home, predicting rooms and their relationships by reading external indicators such as windows, doors, and chimneys. Like John Furriskey in *At Swim*, she comes to understand that the door of a second story chamber rarely shares the same wall with a window. All too quickly, however, the magic goes out of such apprehensions. The means of knowing—grounded in such reasonable arrangements as contiguity, precedence, and sequence—become numbed by routine. The problem is not that things fall apart; the problem is rather that things stand too firmly, limiting and enclosing. *The Third Policeman* seeks to open things up, perhaps trying a door and a window on the same wall several feet above the ground. Like their physical counterparts, the most interesting verbal structures in the novel dramatically deviate from "given arrangements." The novel's physical structures, from Pluck's two-dimensional police station to Fox's extradimensional apartment, set us up for creative distortions in phrase making through which we might reinspire the ways we know and the ways we determine a self.

While considering the problematics of presence, it is important to remember that O'Brien diverts the thrust of his novel away from intellectual solemnity by countering with comic detours. The narrator's interrogation of Mathers rivals the Pooka-Good Fairy dialogues in *At Swim* for its permutations of logic and successfully protects the reader from becoming too involved with any character or "issue." Confronted with the logical contradiction of a dead man drinking tea, the narrator says: "I decided to show unconcern, to talk to the old man and to test his own reality by asking about the black box. . . . Words spilled out of me as if they were produced by machinery" (*TP* 26).

To every question asked—are you dead at present?, do you know where the box is?, do you like weak tea?—Mathers responds with the same "No." Muddled and flustered, the narrator receives assistance from an inner voice which he takes to be his soul and whom, for convenience, he calls "Joe": " 'But do you notice nothing about the way he answers your questions? . . . Do you not see that every reply is in the negative? No matter what you ask him he says No. . . . *Use your imagination*' " (*TP* 27 [italics added]. With Joe's prompting, he begins to reverse his logic, phrasing his questions inside out:

> "Will you refuse to answer a straight question?" I asked.
> "I will not," he replied. (*TP* 28)

To the properly couched, crooked question, Mathers details the method of his manners. He explains that all behavior in life is a response to suggestions or requests from either an inward or an outward party. Admittedly, a few of these suggestions are salutary, but the vast majority are morally detrimental. It follows then, that answering "no" to every request is a simple formula for obviating sin:

> "It was difficult to practice at first and often called for heroism but I persevered and hardly ever broke down completely. It is now many years since I said Yes. I have refused more requests and negatived more statements than any man living or dead. I have rejected, reneged, disagreed, refused and denied to an extent that is unbelievable." (*TP* 30)

O'Brien skillfully keeps it unbelievable by accenting, then

tweaking, the methodology of reason. He ironically refutes what seems to make sense by turning the procedures of order in upon themselves. Joe, the voice of conscience, finds Mathers's schema morally therapeutic, heaping platitudinous praise in the manner of the uncle in *At Swim:* " 'An excellent and original régime. This is all extremely interesting and salutary, every syllable a sermon in itself. Very very wholesome' " (*TP* 30).

Before, however, anyone mistakes Mathers as too exemplary, the old man admits to assorted peccadilloes and misfeasances. It is all a matter of properly structuring the suggestion. When the narrator asks him if he would like a glass of Irish, Mathers answers:

> "Such few friends as I have . . . are usually good enough to arrange such invitations in a way that will enable me to adhere to my system and also accept the whiskey. More than once I have been asked whether I would refuse such things."
> "And the answer is still NO?"
> "Certainly." (*TP* 30)

A similar epistemological enterprise is manhandled later when Martin Finnucane and his band outwit Policeman Fox. The incident plays upon de Selby's treatise on the ancient Celtic practice of " 'throwing a calculation' upon a road":

> In those days wise men could tell to a nicety the dimension of a host which had passed by in the night by looking at their tracks with a certain eye and judging them by their perfection and imperfection, the way each footfall was interfered with by each that came after. In this way they could tell the number of men who had passed, whether they were with horse or heavy with shields and iron weapons, and how many chariots; thus they could say the number of men who should be sent after them to kill them. (*TP* 37–38)

Our narrator, condemned to die (yet again), waits in jail for rescue by Finnucane and his cohorts with wooden prostheses. Fox had scouted the road, observed their tracks, and reported to Policeman Pluck who waits in ambush with eight deputies. The watchdogs of law and order find themselves done in, however, by an imaginative procedural variation. MacCruiskeen explains that the men in blue are bound to find themselves outnumbered and outflanked. Fox has thrown his calculation but the one-legged men have subverted the method of computation:

"Is it for the one-leggèd men he is waiting?"

"Surely yes. But they took a great rise out of Fox. He is certain to get
a severe reprimand from headquarters over the head of it. There is not
seven of them but fourteen. They took off their wooden legs before
they marched and tied themselves together in pairs so that there were
two men for every two legs, it would remind you of Napoleon on the
retreat from Russia, it is a masterpiece of military technocratics." (TP
164)

For me, the most provocative feature of this comedy is its
exploration of "knowledge" as an artifical, vulnerable product of
underlying processes for structuring experience. The narrator's
language reveals that his primary means of making shape—of
knowing—are dictated by chronological, linear arrangements
where the logic of syntax often resembles the human activities of
progeniture, birth, and growth. His cognitive procedures are
based on the systems of timekeeping in which minutes add up to
hours which result in days and form calendar years which ostensibly give shape to a life. Quite obviously, such a means of taming
experience proves nugatory in the wilds of Pluck. The narrator
finds himself no longer able to connect events in a causal series.
Such associations, grounded in the progressive order of logic,
have proven surprisingly inadequate. He faces the task of probing
irregular sorts of coherence, different methods of amalgamation,
modified criteria of communication.[10] If he is to settle himself at
all, he must piece together experience as a recusant, running
counter to cause.

The "dead" man's first tentative response to his dilemma is to
tie sensations together through metaphor. Interestingly, the activity becomes prominent only after the fatal explosion. Here, I
want to reexamine the description of the "something" which happened to upset his comfortable feeling of control: "It was as if the
daylight had changed with unnatural suddenness, as if the tem-
perature of the evening had altered greatly in an instant or as if
the air had become twice as rare or twice as dense as it had been"
(TP 23). "It was as if" is repeated three times here and will become
the primary verbal pattern in the novel. The metaphors "succeed"
one another but, interestingly, each seeks to replace its predecessor rather than to connect with it. Although more dynamic, this
means of making will not quickly or completely satisfy either. The
attempts at verbal correspondence miss the mark because the
standards of comparison are located in sense experience which is
only "valid" in the world of John Divney and the farm—the "real"
world which the narrator has just left. But while the metaphors

are conspicuously vulnerable, they urge further creative acts of invention through which the narrator seeks to locate his presence.

In an essay "On Extravagance," Robert Frost notes: "The extravagance lies in 'it sometimes seems as if.' That would be a good name of a book: 'it sometimes seems as if.' "[11] The extravagance of *The Third Policeman* lies in the narrator's transgressive toying with "as if" 's. Innovative, daring, creative endeavors replace the bankrupt, mechanical procedures of mind and declare their authority in the exhilaration of inventing relationships. The enthusiasm of the narrator's verbal arrangements is only partially dampened by the suspicion that his connections are incomplete; the insuffiency of one "as if" spurs and enables more "as if" 's. The correspondences become increasingly bizarre as he discovers in them the animating charge of composing innovatively. Very simply, his talk becomes much more lively once he is freed from the world of his farm and common sense.

The mad inventions of Policeman MacCruiskeen often prompt provocative metaphors because the narrator finds them "calling into play parts of my brain that I rarely used" (*TP* 69). Listen to him play with MacCruiskeen's peculiar, patent music box:

> MacCruiskeen had been at the dresser a second time and was back at the table with a little black article like a leprechaun's piano with diminutive keys of white and black and brass pipes and circular revolving cogs like parts of a steam engine or the business end of a thrashing-mill. (*TP* 69)

Not surprisingly, MacCruiskeen's instrument produces "an overpowering tremendous silence as if the roof of the room had come down half-way to the floor" (*TP* 69). Obviously, the anxieties over verbal accuracy have given way to an enthusiasm for allying imaginative details. The vital unpredictability of the leprechaun has successfully interfered with the "mechanical" elements of the description, leaving us to enjoy "the business end of a thrashing mill." The "silence," which is "named" by lowering a ceiling, also proves most curious. It calls attention to the extravagant potential of verbal correspondences. The act of making appears looser, freer, enjoyed for its own sake, justifying its presence by its presence.

Frequently, the metaphors run away with their own procedures, celebrating vigorous distortions of what they name. Even Sergeant Pluck gets caught in the act while trying to account for a variation of the standard bicycle configuration:

"The high saddle," said the Sergeant, "was invented by a party called Peters that spent his life in foreign parts riding on camels and other lofty animals—giraffes, elephants and birds that can run like hares and lay eggs the size of the bowl you see in a steam laundry where they keep the chemical water for taking the tar out of men's pants." (*TP* 79)

Here we are treated to a wonderful metaphor which extravagantly strays further and further from its subject. By the time we finish the sentence, we are less concerned with bicycle seats and their inventors, and far more interested in how ostrich eggs generate the particulars of industrial solvents.

The inventive excesses called forth by this environment stimulate the narrator's consideration of the means of knowledge. His excitement with the possibilities of metaphor takes a turn in eternity when he discovers the way naming depends on difference:

> Another door was opened by MacCruiskeen and I was handed a magnifying glass, a very ordinary-looking instrument with a bone handle. I looked at my hand through it and saw nothing that was recognisable. Then I looked at several other things but saw nothing that I could clearly see. MacCruiskeen took it back with a smile at my puzzled eye.
>
> "It magnifies to invisibility," he explained. "It makes everything so big that there is room in the glass for only the smallest particle of it— not enough of it to make it different from any other thing that is dissimilar." (*TP* 136–37)

Like Thomas Pynchon, O'Brien delights in looking at linguistic procedures through the agency of scientific ones. Viewing his hand through this remarkable lens, the narrator sees "nothing" because presence is contingent upon oppositions—however subtle. Disparity determines the outlines which shadow an object or phenomenon, imparting shape. Descending in a lift to the underground place where MacCruiskeen makes his readings, the narrator discovers himself in "eternity," termed so because of its uniform invariability. The policemen point out that down here,

> "The beard does not grow. . . . Your pipe will smoke all day and will still be full and a glass of whiskey will still be there no matter how much of it you drink and it does not matter in any case because it will not make you drunker than your own sobriety. . . ."
>
> "How big is this place?"
>
> "It has no size at all," the Sergeant explained, "because there is no

difference anywhere in it and we have no conception of the extent of its unchanging coequality." (*TP* 133)

The pleasures of language are still involved in the problematics of fiction; while the environment calls for newerfangled verbal formations, all indications still point to instability and insufficiency. But the anxiety of words missing their mark is partially expiated by the thrill of articulating and following their flight. In the subterranean eternity (within the more spacious eternity topside), the narrator often finds himself at a loss for words:

> MacCruiskeen was examining some knobs in a central cabinet. He turned his head and called to me.
> "Come over here," he called, "till I show you something to tell your friends about."
> Afterwards, I saw that this was one of his rare jokes because what he showed me was something that I could tell nobody about, there are no suitable words in the world to tell my meaning. . . . He pressed two red articles like typewriter keys and turned a large knob away from him. At once there was a rumbling noise as if thousands of full biscuit-boxes were falling down a stairs. . . . But what can I say about them? In colour they were not white or black and certainly bore no intermediate colour; they were far from dark and anything but bright. But strange to say it was not their unprecedented hue that took most of my attention. They had another quality that made me watch them wild-eyed, dry-throated and with no breathing. I can make no attempt to describe this quality. It took me hours of thought long afterwards to realise why these articles were astonishing. *They lacked an essential property of all known objects.* I cannot call it shape or configuration since shapelessness is not what I refer to at all. I can only say that these objects, not one of which resembled the other, were of no known dimensions. They were not square or rectangular or circular or simply irregularly shaped nor could it be said that their endless variety was due to dimension dissimilarities. Simply their appearance, if even that word is not inadmissible, was not understood by the eye and was in any event indescribable. That is enough to say. (*TP* 134–35)

Such an imaginatively intriguing description of the indescribable allays any sympathetic alarm or apprehension. Through the narrator's "reticent" efforts, we readers find our attention drawn to the feral possibilities of verbal response accommodating ineffable experience. We encounter one memorable metaphor concerning biscuit-boxes and gravity but, for the most part, the narrator seems to enjoy the opportunity to define by tangential references to absence. We are repeatedly reminded what these objects "lack," are "far from," or are "anything but." Significantly, the sense of incompleteness hastens new verbal efforts. He seems to derive an ambiguous reassurance simply from voicing "inadmissible" words while every attempt reinforces his perception that "there are no suitable words." The comically ironic conclusion, "That is enough to say," begins to resonate, sounding contingent and unreasonable potencies of saying.

The question of whether and how it might be "enough to say" urges us to consider the potential of transgression for confirming presence. Although dead, the storyteller's adventures in the precinct of the absurd revolve around reassuring himself of his existence and safeguarding his life from coming to nothing. "Transgression" may be defined as "the stepping across a barrier or boundary; the violation of an imposed limit." Transgression becomes most interesting here when viewed as an act which tests imposed limits, a performance which translates into style the active interrogation of thresholds. The first transgression, murder, is a comic vehicle for transporting the narrator to a world where other violations become more crucial. A frequently overlooked wanton misdemeanor moves our man into position to commit his most consequential crime—the "re-inscription" of a self.

The salacious scene I refer to is the narrator's amorous assignation with a voluptuous bicycle. To appreciate how an indelicate dalliance between man and machine informs the complicated problems of presence, it is best to review the Atomic Theory as conceived by Policeman Pluck. In response to the narrator's questions, Sergeant Pluck discloses how members of his parish have been slowly swapping their personalities with those of their bicycles:

> "Everything is composed of small particles of itself and they are flying around in concentric circles and arcs and segments and innumerable other geometrical figures too numerous to mention collectively, never standing still or resting but spinning away and darting hither and thither and back again, all the time on the go. These diminutive gentlemen are called atoms." (*TP* 84)

He explains that what we call a "sheep" is actually millions of bits of sheepness constantly on the move, just as each shoe is constituted by exponential enumerations of swirling atoms of shoeness:

"Consecutively and consequentially," he continued, "you can safely infer that you are made of atoms yourself and so is your fob pocket and the tail of your shirt and the instrument you use for taking the leavings out of the crook of your hollow tooth." (*TP* 85)

Once this principle is acknowledged, we are asked to consider what happens when an iron bar is struck by, say, a coal hammer:

"When the wallop falls, the atoms are bashed away down to the bottom of the bar and compressed and crowded there like eggs under a good clucker. After a while in the course of time they swim around and get back at last to where they were. But if you keep hitting the bar long enough and hard enough . . . the bar will dissipate itself away by degrees. . . . Some of the atoms of the bar will go into the hammer and the other half into the table or the stone or the particular article that is underneath the bottom of the bar." (*TP* 85)

Based on this scientific model of atoms and friction, it follows that people who spend a large part of their lives riding iron bicycles over rocky roads inevitably exchange atoms with their vehicles, becoming themselves half-bicycle and creating half-human two-wheelers.

According to Pluck, the validity of the Atomic Theory may be verified by even the simplest daily observations. When a man goes so far as to become more than one-half bicycle, he is frequently seen leaning against a wall on a handlebar/elbow or maintaining his balance with a kickstand/foot propped against a curb. Coincidentally, the man-charged bicycle often conveniently situates it/himself in a cozy corner of the kitchen, near the fire, never far from the family conversation. And although nobody has ever caught one with a mouthful of rasher, suspicious crumbs have been found more than once on the floor around a front tire.

The Sergeant's theorem corroborates the fundamental discrepancy between the reality of words and the world of experience. As the narrator's soul, Joe, affirms: " 'Apparently there is no limit. . . . Anything can be said in this place and it will be true and will have to be believed' " (*TP* 86). Throughout his stay in this realm, the tension between language and empirical experience prompts the narrator to question the validity of his existence. During that first interrogation of Mathers, examined earlier, he realizes: "I did not know my name, did not remember who I was. I was not certain where I had come from or what my business was. . . . I found I was sure of nothing" (*TP* 31).

This is anything but your textbook case of amnesia, however. Divested of a name, he finds himself unable to distinguish his presence from that of the wind, various dogs, or even the American gold watch he claims to have lost. No name means no identity, no originality. On the lighter side, he is warned by Mathers that he can not sign receipts nor may he execute official bank documents. But far more pressing is Sergeant Pluck's explanation of the law of the land: " 'If you have no name you possess nothing and you do not exist and even your trousers are not on you although they look as if they were from where I am sitting' " (*TP* 61–62). Such a predicament is as urgent as it is comic. As Edward Said reminds us: "The novelistic character gains his fictional authority . . . in the desire to escape death . . . in the avoidance of the anonymity of pure negation."[12] It is from this avenue that I would like to approach the one-night stand between man and bicycle, exploring what is essentially a romantic send-up as an attempt to defer death and affirm a potent presence.

Quite late in the novel, after having staved off a knife-wielding robber and been granted a temporary reprieve from the gallows, the anonymous protagonist finds himself with an unexpected opportunity to escape the topsy-turvy wonderland of Policeman Pluck. With the policemen out on an emergency, he discovers a more than ordinary bicycle protruding from a jail cell accidentally left open. As he approaches, he detects "some peculiar quality of shape or personality which gave it distinction." His eye is caught by the "pleasing lustre on its . . . oil bath and a clean sparkle on the rustless spokes and rims." "The perfect proportion of its parts" communicates a "surpassing grace and elegance" which fascinates. Despite a sturdy crossbar, he intuitively senses that he is in the presence of something "ineffably female" (*TP* 169). It seems that Sergeant Pluck has been subject to some perverted peter-peter-pumpkin-eater paranoia and has been keeping a woman-charged bicycle in solitary confinement for his own private service. There is also a hint that the Sergeant likes his play a bit rough; the narrator notices:

> In the back of the small cell was a collection of paint-cans, old ledgers, punctured bicycle tubes, tyre repair outfits and a mass of peculiar brass and leather articles not unlike ornamental horse harness but clearly intended for some wholly different office. (*TP* 167–68)

The passage suggests, with O'Brien's flair for indirection, that these brass and leather goods would be put to good use by the Marquis de Sade.

Recalling the Sergeant's Atomic Theory and his story of a desperate rake who made off with a lady schoolteacher's vehicle, the narrator finds himself overcome with desire:

> I passed my hand with unintended tenderness—sensuously, indeed—across the saddle. . . . I knew that I liked this bicycle more than I had ever liked any other bicycle, better even than I had liked some people with two legs. (*TP* 170)

As his foreplay proceeds, he assumes the linguistic initiative to rename "it" as "she" and "her":

> I liked her unassuming competence, her docility, the simple dignity of her quiet way. She now seemed to rest beneath my friendly eyes like a tame fowl which will crouch submissively, awaiting with out-hunched wings the caressing hand. Her saddle seemed to spread invitingly into the most enchanting of all seats while her two handlebars, floating finely with the wild grace of alighting wings, beckoned to me to lend my mastery for free and joyful journeyings. (*TP* 170–71)

As his passion mounts, he realizes that he and his not-so-coy mistress are about to commence an affair which is more than amatory. Sexual transgression with this bicycle is a significant gesture of defiance directed at Sergeant Pluck and the world he governs. The no-name narrator perceives it as an opportunity to escape the insistence of his eradication, a chance to ride his way into authority:

> In the next moment I was fumbling for the barrack latch with the Sergeant's willing bicycle in my care. We had travelled the passage and crossed the kitchen with the grace of ballet dancers, silent, swift and faultless in our movements, united in the acuteness of our conspiracy. . . . I led the bicycle to the middle of the road, turned her wheel resolutely to the right and swung myself into the centre of her saddle as she moved away eagerly under me in her own time. (*TP* 173)

Through its animated levity, the scene emphasizes the narrator's excitement and pleasure in control. We are encouraged to consider the way his partner's responses to his initiatives generate a heightened and exhilarating self-consciousness:

How can I convey the perfection of my comfort on the bicycle, the completeness of my union with her, the sweet responses she gave me at every particle of her frame? I felt that I had known her for many years and that she had known me and that we understood each other utterly. She moved beneath me with agile sympathy in a swift, airy stride, finding smooth ways among the stony cracks, swaying and bending skilfully to match my changing attitudes. (*TP* 173)

O'Brien is at his best when he teases us into thinking we see our way clear in his novels; often, he then thickens the texture of his prose with passages which convey forking paths. Such is the case here. While this amorous intrigue does reassure the narrator of his potent vitality, it simultaneously becomes the means through which he realizes his presence is a fiction. Pedaling his way home, he finds his journey diverted to the bizarre barracks of Policeman Fox. This station, defying all normal rules of dimension, becomes the arena of a most disquieting interrogation. Questioning his suspect about slipping the hangman's noose, Policeman Fox declares,

"I do not understand your unexpected corporality after the morning on the scaffold."
"I escaped," I stammered.
He gave me long searching glances.
"Are you sure?" he asked.
Was I sure? Suddenly I felt horribly ill as if the spinning of the world in the firmament had come against my stomach for the first time, turning it all to bitter curd. My limbs weakened and hung about me helplessly. Each eye fluttered like a bird's wing in its socket and my head throbbed, swelling out like a bladder at every surge of blood. (*TP* 183)

With absurdly efficacious imagination, the anonymous narrator appropriates the means which insists on his absence. Whenever someone proclaims his "blank anonymity," he counterpunches with meditative, charged metaphors that elicit further oral articulation. Words, which authorize his negation, become the means through which he attempts to mediate an existence.

During an earlier episode in Mathers's house, when the narrator first doubts his existence, he tests his reality through conversation:

I knew that I would go mad unless I got up from the floor and moved and talked. . . . My voice, tremulous at first, grew hard and loud and filled the whole room. I do not remember what I said at the beginning.

I am sure that most of it was meaningless but I was too pleased and reassured at the natural healthy noise of my tongue to be concerned about the words. (*TP* 26)

When Policeman Fox's leading question gravely aggravates the narrator's apprehensions about his "life," he again takes the offensive with a demonstration of voice:

I felt my brains struggling on bravely, tottering, so to speak, to its knees but unwilling to fall completely. I knew that I would be dead if I lost consciousness for one second. . . . I knew that I would have to talk to him and pretend that everything was natural and try perhaps to escape for the last time with my life to the bicycle. (*TP* 183)

He does talk—discussing such matters as strawberry jam, bicycle lamps, and the proper timing for softboiled eggs—eventually talking his way right out of the station. Reunited with his feminine accomplice, he steers a course for home where he hopes to allay his fears through dialogue with John Divney, whose sturdy substance he considers an indisputable fact. Divney, however, suffers a stroke at his entrance and confirms the worst: "He sobbed convulsively where he lay and began to cry and mutter things disjointedly like a man raving at the door of death. It was about me. He told me to keep away. He said I was not there. He said I was dead. . . . I was dead for sixteen years" (*TP* 197).

Paradoxically, our questionable hero responds to the news of his dissolution by composing a novel which amounts to his own obituary. Silence should be the most appropriate expression for a man with no name who does not exist. Yet we have at hand a first-person narrative which tenaciously competes with all assertions of his absence. And the circular complexities of presence hinge on the imaginative indecencies with Policeman Pluck's metal mistress. The pleasures of the saddle generate a vital self-consciousness from which issues the very text we are reading. The confirmation of self in sexual excitement and virility is procreative in that it begets its own re-presentation in language. The sexual transgression of promiscuity with a bicycle intimately informs the verbal transgression of a voice articulating a self as it tells us it is not there.

The intricacies of inscribing presence become more involved when considered with the complicity of the footnotes. The numerous notes act as sportive sidebets within the novel, complicating the play, opening up the game, and freeing the proceedings from predictable direction. As he did in earlier *Comhthrom Feinne* pieces, O'Brien employs the notes most noticeably as agents of disruption. The audience hears the siren call of the small numeral and is drawn to the bottom of the page, interrupting the horizontal progress of the eyes. Once a note gets a grip on our attention, it often wrestles us away from the "primary" text, interposing its own radically different procedures for those of familiar narrative continuity. In chapter XI, we are seduced by a footnote which will ostensibly enhance our understanding of de Selby's narcolepsy. It happens to run on for seven pages, moving itself through one digression after another, until we find ourselves contemplating not sleep, but Hatchjaw's Hamburg career as a brothel-keeper's pimp. By the time we flip back several pages to the opening of the chapter, we have lost our way in a maze of directional choices. The only way out of this dizzying labyrinth is to begin the chapter again, determined to fix our gaze on the larger print at the top half of the page.*

While entangled in the footnotes, we recognize (and, one hopes, smile at) the format of academic criticism and intellectual infighting. Many of the notes are deliberately tedious, comprising ridiculous commentaries on inconsequential matters. They spoof the conventions of learned impersonality which often overdo their "characteristic reconditeness and obscurity" (*TP* 145). And, most significantly, they parody their own procedures, exaggerating the proclivity of any text to beget various subtexts.

De Selby's *Golden Hours* (with the last two pages missing) has sired a slew of critical tracts which are directly responsible for the novel we are reading. The narrator alludes to the unusual concatenation of circumstances early on: "Perhaps it is important in the story I am going to tell to remember that it was for de Selby I committed my first serious sin. It was for him that I committed my greatest sin" (*TP* 9).

He begins his literary career by pilfering a first edition of de Selby's *Golden Hours* and subsequently murders Mathers to finance the publication of his "definitive 'De Selby Index'." He explains to John Divney that his powerful book redresses previous critical inaccuracies: "In fact it contained much that was entirely new and proof that many opinions widely held about de Selby and his theories were misconceptions based on misreadings of his works" (*TP* 14). The whole commentary business gets to be a

---

*This game is quite like the one played by Laurence Sterne. Chapter IX of *The Third Policeman* recalls chapter XX of *Tristram Shandy*. The footnotes in chapter IX usurp authority, employing more words than the narrative.

Quaker Oats game like the novel-within-a-novel-within-a-novel-within-a-novel framing of *At Swim*. Our narrator will emend Henderson's article concerning Le Fournier's treatise on Hatchjaw's critique of de Selby.

Besides fracturing the narrative and questioning critical procedures (like the one I am engaged in now), the footnotes interestingly interact with the anonymous protagonist's quest to establish presence. Since the notes refer to his narrative, they confirm his voice—and ostensibly a presence behind that voice—as residing in a fairly stable text. The footnotes utilize an antecedent text as a springboard for their own acrobatics, yet they paradoxically affirm the authority of the prior, more primary, text even as they attempt to challenge or supplant. The issue is never plain and rarely simple, however, and O'Brien enjoys complicating the proceedings just when we think we have it figured out. Again, he leads us in opposite directions. Some of the footnotes suggest that language might be merely a self-enclosed system of signs referring to other signifiers behind which lie nothing. The suggestion is, of course, backhanded and anything but conclusive. The first notes of the novel arise from de Selby's curious recommendations for appropriate housing. His irritation with interiors and distaste for confinement are supposedly responsible for his formidable treatise on " 'habitats', crude drawings of which may still be seen in the pages of the Country Album" (*TP* 21). De Selby's tract carefully diagrams and extensively discusses two types of superior lodging: "roofless 'houses' and 'houses' without walls." These structures serve as the foundation for a provocative critique:

[3]Le Fournier, the reliable French commentator (in *De Selby—l'Énigme de l'Occident*) has put forward a curious theory regarding these "habitats." He suggests that de Selby, when writing the *Album*, paused to consider some point of difficulty and in the meantime engaged in the absent-minded practice known generally as "doodling," then putting his manuscript away. The next time he took it up he was confronted with a mass of diagrams and drawings which he took to be the plans of a type of dwelling he always had in mind and immediately wrote many pages explaining the sketches. (*TP* 21–22)

The suggestion here is that signs—whether doodles or words—may be arbitrary labels referring back to and enabling further unreliable signifiers. The possibility obviously interests O'Brien for he toys with it further in a footnote concerning the de Selby "Codex":

> [2] The reader will be familiar with the storms which have raged over this most tantalising of holographic survivals. The "Codex" (first so-called by Bassett in his monumental *De Selby Compendium*) is a collection of some two thousand sheets of foolscap closely hand-written on both sides. The signal distinction of the manuscript is that not one word of the writing is legible. Attempts made by different commentators to decipher certain passages which look less formidable than others have been characterised by fantastic divergencies, not in the meaning of the passages (of which there is no question) but in the brand of nonsense which is evolved. One passage, described by Bassett as being "a penetrating treatise on old age" is referred to by Henderson (biographer of Bassett) as "a not unbeautiful description of lambing operations on an unspecified farm." (*TP* 145)

Only the most myopic could miss the humor of "retrieving" meaning through the "re-presentation" of the illegible. Some contemporary critics might even recognize their own complicity in the inspection and exegesis of four thousand pages of unreadable black marks. O'Brien does indicate that language may signify empty absurdity but his manner is always playfully comic. The self-conscious levity of his delivery reminds us not to over-interpret and steers us away from constructing grand "issues" from his prose. I think O'Brien would essentially agree with R. P. Blackmur when he says: "The shock and virtue of nonsense is this: it compels us to scrutinize words in such a way that we see the enormous ambiguity in the substance of every phrase, every image, every word."[13] Like Oedipa Maas's notion of metaphor in *The Crying of Lot 49*, the prospect of nothing behind the language is both "a thrust at truth and a lie."[14] It all depends on where you stand, and O'Brien gets around quite a bit. With still more nonsense, he spotlights, temporarily, the substantiality of language and offers the possibility of confirming a voice, an identity, a presence through a text.

The quarrelling of two antagonistic de Selbian critics sets the stage for this wonderfully imaginative theoretical digression. The "customary sarcasm" of the Frenchman du Garbandier is often offset by rejoinder from "the credulous Kraus" and the two rivals establish a long history of mixing it up with words:

> It is now commonly accepted that Hatchjaw was convinced that the name "du Garbandier" was merely a pseudonym adopted for his own ends by the shadowy Kraus. It will be recalled that Bassett took the opposite view, holding that Kraus was a name used by the mordant Frenchman for spreading his slanders in Germany. It may be observed

that neither of these theories is directly supported by the writings of either commentator: du Garbandier is consistently virulent and defamatory while much of Kraus' work, blemished as it is by his inaccurate attainments in scholarship, is not at all unflattering to de Selby. Hatchjaw . . . states his conviction that Kraus was making a considerable fortune by publishing tepid refutations of du Garbandier's broadsides. This suggestion is not without colour because, as he points out, Kraus had extremely elaborate books on the market—some containing expensive plates—within an incredibly short time of the appearance of a poisonous volume under the name of du Garbandier. (*TP* 168)

The comic confusions here are further complicated in a footnote which suggests that Hatchjaw and Bassett could themselves be one-in-the-same, arguing the Kraus/du Garbandier, du Garbandier/Kraus controversy with a similar self-justifying end in mind.[15]

All this nonsense sportively suggests that establishing a voice through words testifies to a presence sounding and arranging the words. If the presence is the fiction of an invented voice, so much the better. The matter is far more provocative if du Garbandier is indeed a construct of Kraus because the fictive voice of du Garbandier acts as an obstacle against which the textual voice of Kraus may push. This brand of nonsense points to the way all authors—however indirectly—establish a textual presence by writing against perceived or invented resistances.

The footnotes, then, temporarily affirm the narrator's presence as they work off his voice while it forms itself in the primary text. But his substantiality remains intriguingly ambiguous because the narrative itself functions as a resistive response to Pluck's and Mathers's declarations of his absence. His narrative, this novel, becomes the theater where an absent storyteller rhetorically attempts to enact his presence. The activity is as courageous as it is complicated because the performance forever remains unaffirmed. From the actor's point of view, the curtain falls as it rose—to silence. Ironically and interestingly, the performance is never "over"; the role and the existence it tries to confirm remain incomplete, doomed to eternal repetition. Through sportive verbal transgression, however, *The Third Policeman* roundly declares that dead men do tell tales and, presumably, even find time in eternity to write them down.

5

The Hard Life and *The Dalkey Archive:* The Craft of Seeming Pedestrian

> I considered it desirable that he should know nothing about me but it was even better if he knew several things which were quite wrong.
>
> —*The Third Policeman*

In 1961, Flann O'Brien's long-awaited "second" novel, *The Hard Life,* finally appeared in print. Since *The Third Policeman* remained languishing in a drawer and *An Beal Bocht* was cast in Gaelic, *The Hard Life* was greeted by most as the second book by the author of *At Swim-Two-Birds.* The twenty-odd year wait seems to have whetted the enthusiasm of readers and critics alike. The novel sold out in Dublin within two days, and reviewers, especially in England, praised it with gusto.[1]

Since then, however, we have seen an about-face in the ranks of commentators. The critical line, nowadays, is that O'Brien spent his talent and played himself out writing his Myles na Gopaleen column for the *Irish Times.* Both *The Hard Life* and *The Dalkey Archive* (1964) are often taken lightly as enervated, end-of-career efforts by a writer who once had good stuff.[2] However, O'Brien's unpublished letters to his friends Niall Montgomery and Niall Sheridan, to his agents at A. M. Heath, Patience Ross and Mark Hamilton, and to his publisher during the 1960's, Timothy O'Keeffe, reveal that both novels are intended as experiments in subterfuge. *The Hard Life* masquerades as a tame, straightforward novel as it explores how discourses collapse, sounding only a desperately squalid void. *The Dalkey Archive* promotes an intriguingly inconsistent narrator who covertly interferes with prior literary storytellers to reverse narrative valences with which readers have traditionally been drawn.

In *The Hard Life,* O'Brien works with readily recognized fictional

142

patterns in order to dismantle them. The text suggests that the mimetic novel—which attempts to simulate our daily world even as it rivals and augments it—is most inauthentic precisely when readers accept it as "realistic." In a letter to Timothy O'Keeffe, O'Brien took pains to promote his masking: "*The Hard Life* is a very important book and very funny. Its apparently pedestrian style is delusive."[3] Niall Sheridan, O'Brien's close friend and trusted commentator, praised this self-effacing performance as it was in progress: "The atmosphere of unbelievable squalor has a powerful fascination and the very cunning simplicity of the style puts it across perfectly."[4]

The "cunning simplicity" of style is definitely intended. It would be a mistake to read the novel for thematic plot development. "Narrative" is in fact faked, with *The Hard Life* exposing itself as a series of scenes loosely linked by cardboard character development. The novel centers, rather, on the pedantic verbal tennis matches between the uncle, Mr. Collopy, and the neighboring German priest, Father Kurt Fahrt, S.J. Their respective "pedestrian styles" compete and interact, building networks of discourse which ironically affirm the absences they seek to counter.

Writing to his agent, Mark Hamilton, at A. M. Heath & Company, O'Brien emphasizes the centrality of the periphrastic dialogue in this novel:

> Everything was done with deliberation, the characters illuminating themselves and each other by their outlandish behavior and preposterous conversations. . . . A few people here whose opinion I value have seen the MS and all are really impressed, particularly by the Collopy—Father Fahrt dialogues.[5]

Obviously, the author is pleased with himself. Not as obvious, however, are the ways through which conversations self-reflexively expose language as fields of incomplete, volatile substitution. The two contenders frequently spend an evening in Collopy's kitchen, engaged in "sapient colloquy" like talking heads. Some readers are put off that there is scarcely a "likable person" in the novel.[6] However, *The Hard Life* never invites us to consider characters as people. Characters are presented as voices employing distinct rhetorical modes which inevitably reveal a pregnant lack. The omissions which conversation tries to circumscribe are only indirectly and incompletely defined by the failure of words. Like the young boy in Joyce's "The Sisters," the reader remains perplexed and intrigued by what's not said.

The relationship between language and the want it seeks to replace is similar to one Collopy notices in the house of the clergy. When he decides that his nephew Finbarr is ready to attend school, Collopy escorts him to the Christian Brothers' establishment on Synge Street. As they wait for Brother Gaskett in an anteroom of the rectory, the uncle noses around the encompassing odor of sanctification: "They say piety has a smell, Mr. Collopy mused, half to himself. It's a perverse notion. What they mean is only the absence of the smell of women" (HL 23).[7] A like correspondence motivates the voices of Collopy and Fahrt. As we make our way through their comic nonsense, we confront a disquieting want which makes itself more insistent as we proceed.

Each voice displays a prominent, easily recognizable manner of selecting and combining words. Collopy's sound is that of cliché-ridden, vituperative "Paddy Whack." To the platitudinous provincialisms of the uncle in At Swim, he adds the "bought-and-paid-for-Paddy" talk which O'Brien so objected to in Abbey Theatre productions.[8] Collopy's moral modest proposals are littered with folksy Irish expressions such as "pishrogues," "gorawars," "looderamawn," "gobshite," and "smahan." Father Fahrt's field of discourse flaunts the well-known Jesuitical dodge. He deflects Collopy's onslaughts with memorized catechistical responses, banal metaphors, and his Order's own brand of "rigorous" logic. Although the two assume they converse, each ultimately talks to himself, trying to assure and invigorate an existence enclosed by claustrophobic formulations. Their friendly disputations traverse the same old ground wearing, not a path, but a trench which determines the course of their counsel as it walls in their horizons.

Their kitchen contentions often canvass Biblical scholarship and church history in an attempt to vitalize something they only vaguely intuit as exhaused. They refer to and "revise" religious traditions, seeking to secure a stable, coherent system of knowing. Ironically, they recover nothing but verbal bedlam:

> Did I hear you right when you said "humble," Father? An humble Jesuit would be like a dog without a tail or a woman without a knickers on her. Did you ever hear tell of the Spanish Inquisition?
>
> I did of course, Father Fahrt said unperturbed. The faith was in danger in Spain. If a bad wind will blow out your candle, you will protect your candle with the shade of your hand. Or perhaps some sort of cardboard shield.
>
> Cardboard shield? Mr. Collopy echoed scornfully. Well damn the cardboard shields the Dominicans used in Spain, those blood-stained bowsies.

My own Order, Father Fahrt said modestly, was under the thumb of the Suprema in Madrid and yet I make no complaint. . . .

You have a smart answer for everything. "Do you believe in the true faith?" "No." "Very well. Eight hundred lashes." If that's the Catholic Church for you, is it any wonder there was a Reformation? Three cheers for Martin Luther!

Father Fahrt was shocked.

Collopy, please remember that you belong to the true fold yourself. That talk is scandalous. . . .

Eight hundred lashes for telling the truth according to your conscience? What am I talking about—the holy friars in Spain propagated the true faith by driving red hot nails into the backs of unfortunate Jewmen.

Nonsense.

And scalding their testicles with boiling water.

You exaggerate, Collopy.

And ramming barbed wire or something of the kind up where-you-know. And all *A.M.D.G.* to use your own motto, Father. (*HL* 35–37)

Throughout the novel, the reader enjoys overhearing privy discussions of torture and disease, urine and vomit. Critics, however, frequently misconstrue these references which feature pain and scatology. First, the comedy of such excessiveness is often overlooked. The context and comportment of learned disputation is wonderfully deflated by imaginative, gratuitous details such as "a woman without a knickers," "red hot nails," and "unfortunate Jewmen." The use of these particulars (clichés and barely signifying) seems to free Collopy from any stultifying adherence to fact. And his frenetic irreverence progressively builds on itself with cadences like "something of the kind" generating deferential ambiguities like "up where-you-know." The humor here recalls the "Description of a social evening at the Furriskey household" in *At Swim*, where talk of piles, bedsores, blackheads, and hunchbacks assists the polite teatime banter about crockery, the "pianofurty," and passing-the-sugar.

In a letter to his literary agent at Heath, O'Brien awards himself a backhanded compliment on the fulsome flavor of the novel: "I do not think this is a very funny book, though no dog is a judge of his own vomit. It is old, elegant, nostalgic piss. . . ."[9] In fact, without his canine mask, O'Brien thought the book hilarious and savored all the praise Niall Sheridan could heap concerning its comic qualities. The scurrilous vocabulary, however, is not meant to be merely vulgar; the diction acts as a catalyst for deflation, hurrying the novel's momentum toward emptiness.

In addition, the pageantry of sordidness has prompted comparisons with Joyce which often prove reductive. Clissmann states: "The chief reference to Joyce comes, however, in the subtitle, *An Exegesis of Squalor.* The book is an attempt to sum up the atmosphere of *Dubliners* and *A Portrait of the Artist*, with sly digs on the way at *Ulysses*."[10] Loose, diffuse generalities such as this victimize Joyce as well as O'Brien. Certainly, Joyce never shied away from dirty ditches or "dog in the blanket," but he would never claim a monopoly on life's sordid tides. Irish mythology and folklore have long enjoyed a tradition of artistically handling physical messes.

One of the more pregnant kitchen conversations provides a better commentary on the novel's telling squalor. As Collopy and Fahrt try to refashion a comforting version of the Garden of Eden, Finbarr's brother, Manus, interrupts his betters:

> Excuse me, Father Fahrt. . . .
> Yes, Manus?
> The wife of Adam in the Garden of Eden was Eve. She brought forth two sons, Cain and Abel. Cain killed Abel but afterwards in Eden he had a son named Henoch. Who was Cain's wife?
> Well, Father Fahrt said, there has been disputation on that point. . . .
> Even if Eve had a daughter not mentioned, she would be Cain's sister. If she hadn't, then Cain must have married his own mother. Either way it seems to be a bad case of incest.
> What sort of derogatory backchat is that you are giving out of you about the Holy Bible? Mr. Collopy bellowed. (*HL* 54)

We immediately relish "the brother" 's appropriation of Fahrt's logical method, his turning the story of Adam and Eve into a tale of illicit romance. Manus's "innocent query" suggests that the verbal intercourse between the two grown-ups is just as incestuous. More significantly, the scene points up the way all conversation in the novel tries to perform as exegesis, countering the squalor of nonmeaning. Exegesis attempts to "show the way," to secure coherence, and to compensate for a lack of meaning by making order. Ironically, the disordered incompleteness which talk attempts to counteract becomes more troubling and elusive with each explanation. Words expose themselves as insufficient substitutes for the void they try to fill. All communication remains inconclusive and functions metaphorically like Mr. Collopy's ceramic liquor receptacle:

> On the floor beside Mr. Collopy's chair was what was known as "the crock." It was in fact a squat earthenware container, having an ear on

each side, in which the Kilbeggan Distillery marketed its wares. The Irish words for whiskey—*Uisge Beatha*—were burnt into its face. This vessel was, of course, opaque and therefore mysterious; one could not tell how empty or full it was, nor how much Mr. Collopy had been drinking. (*HL* 31–32)

Conversations here amount to comic "crocks"—impaired, mysterious, opaque vessels which hide an interesting emptiness inimical to words.

This theme of avoidance is saved from being staid, however, by O'Brien's unflagging posture of play. "Avoidance" becomes a diverting escapade when it is literalized with respect to women. The two philosophers often descant antiphonally and at length on Collopy's "work," his "urgent mission." The uncle is obviously obsessed with some arcane corporal work of mercy designed to benefit women but "as usual, the subject under discussion was never named" (*HL* 31).

Writing to A. M. Heath, O'Brien again provides a salient, semiserious critique: "two of the comics in it are Father Kurt Fahrt, S.J. and our Holy Father the Pope, but there is absoutely no irreverence. The theme, never specifically mentioned though obvious to any reader, is the most preposterous in all the literature of the earth."[11] Despite the innocent "who me?" posture, O'Brien's irreverence becomes more blatant the longer the "theme" remains hidden, the longer his characters' linguistic references miss their mark. As readers, all we know is that Collopy is infuriated over some portentous matter which he believes the municipal authorities ought to rectify. He constantly blames the Dublin Corporation for the dismal state of affairs and has marshaled a committee of concerned citizens to agitate for the cause. Eventually, near the end of the novel, we find out that his allusive enterprise is the establishment of women's public lavatories in Dublin. Like Leopold Bloom, Collopy laments the lack of fair play. If caught short, a man can always duck into a pub; a woman, however, has to hunt for a cakeshop to "settle my hat straight."[12] More often than not, the dialogic pluralities collapse into clichéd contradictions: "Decent people should look after women—isn't that right? The weaker sex. Didn't God make them the same as he made you and me, Father?" (*HL* 42). The reader's uncertainty and pleasure derive from O'Brien's linguistic play. We are constantly kept guessing, asked to feel our way through a peculiar penumbra of verbal substitution.

Collopy and Fahrt frequently shift the focus of their discussions, obliquely tacking with camouflaged transitions:

Tell me this, Father. Would you say it's *natural* for a woman to have children?

Provided she is married in a union blessed by the Church—yes. Most natural and most desirable. It is a holy thing to raise children to the greater glory of God. Your catechism will tell you that. The celibate and priestly state is the holiest of all but the station of the married man is not ignoble. And of course the modest married woman is the handmaid of the Lord.

Very good, Mr. Collopy said warmly. Then tell me this. Is the other business natural?

Certainly. Our bodies are sacred temples. It is a function.

Very well. What name have you for the dirty ignoramuses who more or less ban that function?

It is, ah, thoughtlessness, Father Fahrt said in his mildest voice. Perhaps if a strong hint were dropped. . .

If a hint were dropped, Mr. Collopy exploded. *If a hint were dropped!* (HL 34)

First hearing this, we are far from sure if or how they have moved from the Church's stand on procreation. Such phrases as "other business" and "that function" as well as ingratiating ambiguities like "Our bodies are sacred temples" warily and deftly circle what is missing. O'Brien's game, of course, is to delay the disclosure as long as possible; consequently, solutions to the problem are proffered with inventive equivocation:

Why not have the whole scandalous situation denounced from the pulpit?

Oh . . . dear. . . . The Church's first concern, Collopy, is with faith and morals. Their application to everyday life is pretty wide but I fear your particular problem is far, far outside the pale. (HL 39–40)

Fahrt's reference to "the pale" raises an interesting paradoxical metaphor. In one sense, the conversations enact a performance of words circling a lack. But Collopy's and Father Fahrt's talk might seem more limited if it were considered as constituting "the pale," the fenced-off area encompassed by and determined by absence. In both senses, however, the attraction of all oral substitutes is the light punning way hints are dropped.

After extensive thought, the good Father does manage to prescribe a cure which would conform with Church policy: prayer. However, Mr. Collopy is more the man of science than faith. He is sure that the Lord Mayor will be more moved by measurement, data, and documentation than he will be by any dose of celestial grace. With the help of his committee, he devises a scheme whereby concerned ladies will utilize technological apparatus to gather evidence:

> There now Rafferty, didn't I tell you, what? That articles on the table is a clinical hydrometer. As we agreed, you are to bring it to Mrs. Flaherty. Tell her to take careful readings day and night for a fortnight from next Saturday at noon. And keep the most meticulous records.
>
> Oh, I understand how important that is, Mr. Collopy. And I'll make Mrs. Flaherty understand.
>
> In these modern times, you are damn nothing unless you can produce statistics. Columns and columns of figures, readings and percentages. Suppose they set up a Royal Commission on this thing? Where would we be if we couldn't produce our certified statistics? What would we look like in the witness chair? . . . And when Mrs. Flaherty has given us her readings, we will give the next fortnight to Mrs. Clohessy. (HL 96–97)

It must be remembered that congregating compatible incidents like this is more than a bit misleading. What seem like obvious references after the fact are actually imaginatively puzzling insinuations while read. Talk of Collopy's project is never sustained for long. The matter is usually alluded to, then quickly dropped, remaining incomplete, underground.

This comedy of obfuscation comes to a head as Collopy and Fahrt travel to Rome for a private audience with Pope Pius X. Their visit is designed to effect a miraculous cure for Collopy's physical afflictions, but Cardinal Baldini inadvertently redirects their purpose with his appraisal of the Pontiff:

> the man you are going to meet is the Pope of the Poor and the humble. In any way he can help them, he always does.
>
> Is that a fact? Collopy said. (HL 134)

The papal pomp and circumstance, complete with Swiss Guards and the Fisherman's Ring, are about to get soiled with supplications for metropolitan conveniences. The humor, however, acquires its charge not so much from incongruity, as in the suggestive dexterity of presentation. Collopy knows no Latin or Italian and the Pope no English, so Monsignor Cahill acts as interpreter between the shepherd and his flock. Manus, who reports the incident in a letter back to Finbarr, is seated too far away to hear any of the whispered exchanges. He is only privy to the Pope's startled facial reactions and his foreign-tongued rejoinders:

At the time I had no idea, of course, what the subject of the audience had been or what had been said in Latin or Italian by the Pope. It was only when I interviewed Monsignor Cahill the following day that I got the information I have set down here. I asked him what the subject of Mr. Collopy's representations were. He said he had given his word of honor that he would not disclose this to anybody. (*HL* 139)

The interview is transcribed as a crazy, one-sided conversation which we cannot resist trying to complete. The reader has to work backwards from verbal pauses, rhythms, and inflections the way one might if he or she were to overhear half of a telephone conversation from a distance which blurred the words. Preliminary greetings over, Collopy gets down to business:

> (After a little more desultory conversation Mr Collopy said something in a low voice which I did not catch. Monsignor Cahill instantly translated. The Pope seemed startled. . . .)
> THE POPE
> Che cosa sta dicendo questo poveretto?
> *What is this poor child trying to say?*
> MONSIGNOR CAHILL spoke.
> THE POPE
> E tocco? Nonnunquam urbis nostrae visitentium capitibus affert vaporem. Dei praesidium hujus infantis amantissimi invocare velimus.
> *Is this child in his senses? Sometimes the heat of our city brings a vapour into the heads.* . . .
>
> *FATHER FAHRT* spoke.
> THE POPE
> Ma questo è semplicemente monstruoso. Neque hoc nostrum officium cum concilii urbani officio est confundendum.
> *But this is monstrous. Nor should our office be confused with that of a city council.* . . .
>
> Bona mulier fons gratiae. Attamen ipsae in parvularum rerum suarum occupationibus verrentur. Nos de tantulis rebus consulere non decet.
> *A good woman is a fountain of grace. But it is themelves whom they should busy about their private little affairs. It is not seemly to consult us on such matters.* (HL 135–38)

The interview continues for quite some time, compounding its complications and picking up momentum the longer the "matter" remains verbally veiled. The suppliants are finally dismissed on something less than a benedictory note: "As a matter of fact the

Pope told us all to go to hell. He threatened to silence Father Fahrt" (*HL* 133).

The entire sequence derives its vitality from the way silences are verbally evoked: "holy discourse" engages our imaginative "sound of sense" as it embarrassingly envelops the unmentioned. The Latin and Italian delivery really animates the humor because even the middling scholar and the infrequent churchgoer have learned to respond to such vibrations deferentially. The sound of liturgical rhythms freighted with "bus," "mus," "ium," "rum" endings lends an air of reverential dignity to the proceedings. These passages charm and captivate as the incensed sermonets eventually disclose themselves as so much "papal bull" for skirting the private little affairs of women. Niall Sheridan congratulates his friend: "the final episode in Rome (including the papal audience and your man's fantastic death) is one of the most uproarious comic climaxes I can remember."[13] Sheridan is correct in pointing out the episodic character of the novel and the placement of climax. The uproar, however, centers not on invented plot but on the tumult fostered by language which just won't sit still.

Subsequently, matters quickly resolve themselves in a manner which underscores the absurdity of the plot. Collopy dies in Rome but leaves a will with a codicil which compensates for the dereliction of the Dublin Corporation. A large portion of his estate is earmarked for a characteristically peculiar trust fund. Resting in peace in Rome, Collopy arranges for women to do something similar on Dublin streets:

> The Trust will erect and maintain three establishments which the testator calls rest rooms. There will be a rest room at Irishtown, Sandymount, at Harold's Cross and at Phibsborough. Each will bear the word PEACE very prominently on the door and each will be under the patronage of a saint—Saint Patrick, Saint Jerome and Saint Ignatius. Each of these establishments will bear a plaque reading, for instance, "THE COLLOPY TRUST—Rest Room of Saint Jerome." (*HL* 152–53)

O'Brien's consequential comedy underscores how, even in death, Collopy's language eludes him. What self-respecting Dublin woman would seek rest or peace in a room that sounds as if it were composed of saintly urinals?

Through its pose as realistic fiction, *The Hard Life* rebukes the reader looking for authenticity in the novel. Focusing on dialogue, it investigates "communication" as interestingly enjoined by a void beyond words. An English character in another novel once said of Irish talk:

> If the essence of conversation is communication, then the Irish failed the test, dealing as they did in evasion and obfuscation. Irish conversation was like one of those Celtic designs in the Book of Kells made up of a simple form like a serpent that tied itself into thousands of ornamental knots before finally eating its own tail.[14]

Prejudicial and incorrect in general, these remarks score well when applied to *The Hard Life*. The conversations of Collopy and Fahrt constantly miss the mark, but their failures comically enable further intricate failures. The pleasure of this text is hearing the formation of various verbal knots and tasting, imaginatively, the tang of the tale.

Although it too understates its subversiveness, *The Dalkey Archive* is a much livelier, more free-wheeling novel than *The Hard Life*. Once again, O'Brien practices upon literary processes and procedures, but here we find him operating with new instruments. In his last completed novel, O'Brien employs a most unusual third-person narrator, a master of revels who subtly interferes with our accustomed methods of reading. This histrionic shaping sensibility focuses on parodies of antecedent narrative tropes and literary traditions of "redemption," especially the notions of artistic redemption nominated in Joyce's *A Portrait of the Artist as a Young Man*.

Commentators usually focus on one of two features of the novel, neither of which proves especially fruitful. One inclination is to read *Dalkey* as a "revision" of *The Third Policeman* because O'Brien reuses some names and a skit from his dormant manuscript composed twenty-four years earlier. We do encounter De Selby and Pluck again (more than slightly altered), and Sergeant Fottrell's Mollycule Theory recalls the Atomic Theory of the earlier Sergeant Pluck. But textual comparisons do not take us very far; the dispositions of the two novels differ sharply. Where *The Third Policeman* disturbs with its nightmarish black comedy, *The Dalkey Archive* delights as a burlesque which never takes itself too seriously.

A second impulse is to make too much of O'Brien "resurrecting" James Joyce and placing him as a character in this fiction. Surely, O'Brien is getting even with the master, reducing the novelist to a function within a novel. And the business is good for a few laughs, especially when Joyce claims that Sylvia Beach concocted *Ulysses* and when the celebrated exile winds up joining the Jesuits as an underwear repair man. O'Brien rewrites Joyce more tellingly, however, with a subdued parody of Stephen Dedalus.

Surprisingly, no critics emphasize what I consider to be a central innovation in O'Brien's writing. As late as three months before publication, O'Brien decided to alter his strategy strikingly, switching from first person to a third-person presentation. All of his other novels use a first-person perspective, and *Dalkey* had been composed in the same way. Yet, at the last minute, O'Brien chose to radically revamp his point of view, deviating in a manner which dramatically energizes the novel. In letters to Timothy O'Keeffe, Mark Hamilton, and Niall Montgomery, O'Brien details his strategy. In November 1963, he writes to O'Keeffe: "My ultimate plan is to excoriate the MS ruthlessly, cutting short here and rebuilding there, giving the book precision and occasionally the beauty of jewelled ulcers. It must above all be bitterly funny. The first person sing. must be made into a more awful toad than now."[15] He reports to Mark Hamilton during January 1964: "A fundamental reform is the annihilation of the first person singular as narrator; this character must not only become a more obnoxious pest than at present but also third person singular and very third class."[16] On the same day, he writes to Montgomery: "Apart from annihilating first pers. sing. narrator, I am also making him give up drink early in the book. That will be one small factor in making him even a more obnoxious prig than he is."[17] O'Brien and Montgomery had an unusual manner of correspondence. On letters sent to him, Montgomery would respond with marginal notes in hand and add holograph pages, sometimes longer than the original. On O'Brien's letter cited above, Montgomery replies: "I agree with your further emasculation of the narrator but he is not the principal character."[18]

As late as 6 January 1964, O'Brien radically alters the major thrust of the novel. The former "protagonist," Mick Shaughnessey, is significantly demoted and O'Brien begins developing a new third-person narrator as a most provocative storytelling sensibility. His deliberately inconsistent self-consciousness moves the reader through contrapositive modes of encountering a text, and his pervasive parody of his own and other narrators' methods affords us the proper perspective from which to view this pseudo-*bildungsroman*.

The novel commences in a curious fashion:

> Dalkey is a little town maybe twelve miles south of Dublin, on the shore. It is an unlikely town, huddled, quiet, pretending to be asleep. Its streets are narrow, not quite self-evident as streets and with meetings which seem accidental. Small shops look closed but are open. Dalkey looks like an humble settlement which must, a traveller feels, be next door to some place of the first importance and distinction. And it is—vestibule of a heavenly conspection. (*DA* 7)[19]

Except for that last phrase, the description seems innocent enough, amicably introducing the reader to a quaint, friendly place. But the opening line, with its colloquial "maybe," tentatively takes the first step in a journey of uncertainty. Dalkey, and the proceedings associated with it, presents appearances which prove subtly misleading. The town, "pretending to be asleep," displays open shops which "look closed." Its streets, "not quite self-evident as streets," "seem" to encounter one another by chance. In general, the area exudes an "humble" self-effacing air which gently misinforms. Like the town, and through his descriptions of it, the narrative voice plays games with "seeming." This narrator toys with our semiwilling suspension of disbelief, inviting our intimate participation in novelistic events, yet, simultaneously, warning us to step back if we want to see the real show. Often seeming to travel in two directions at once, he postures as a neutral, disinterested observer and, at the same time, flaunts his performance as a literary ringmaster.

The second paragraph begins the theatrics. Taking a cue from the odd collocation, "vestibule of a heavenly conspection," the narrator marches front stage and dramatically gesticulates to the scenery which serves as his backdrop: "Behold it. Ascend a shaded, dull, lane-like way, *per iter,* as it were, *tenebricosum,* and see it burst upon you as if a curtain had been miraculously whisked away. Yes, the Vico Road" (*DA* 7).

The colloquial, inviting tone of the first paragraph is immediately countered by a voice of high-handed histrionics as the imperative "Behold" jars us with its strangeness. Most readers are distanced from the word as much by art as by the passage of time. In *A Midsummer Night's Dream,* Lysander may explain why "The course of true love never did run smooth" by exclaiming that love is like sudden lightning: "And ere a man hath power to say 'Behold!' / The jaws of darkness do devour it up: . . ."[20] Likewise, in the story of Christ's nativity, celestial spirits may placate the shepherds by announcing: "Fear not: for, behold, I bring you good tidings of great joy, which shall be to all people."[21] But when a novelistic character commands us to "Behold" we can be sure that his next injunction, "Ascend," really means take a giant step backwards. He directs us to take a look at his language, noticing the phony mixture of Latin and English as well as his gaudy display of the overworked "curtain" metaphor.

After this moment of self-display, however, the storyteller discreetly recedes from view by altering his voice. He redirects our attention to the "natural" environment of Dalkey by modulating his diction and tempering his tone. The reader is soothingly coerced to forget that he is reading; instead, we are prompted to participate, to envision the topography and geography of the place. Through the unassuming voice of a transparent medium, we are placed on a high grassy hill where our gaze is directed across enchanting Killiney Bay to an idyllic picture of gentle clouds.

But just as we begin to be lulled into the enjoyable state of novelistic imperviousness, the narrator reemerges as a Puckish shaping sensibility. He sets up agonistic verbal formations which forcibly remind us that we have a book in our hands:

> And to the right? Monstrous arrogance: a mighty shoulder of granite climbing ever away, its overcoat of furze and bracken embedded with stern ranks of pine, spruce, fir and horse-chestnut, with further on fine clusters of slim, meticulous eucalyptus—the whole a dazzle of mildly moving leaves, a farrago of light, colour, haze and copious air, a wonder that is quite vert, verdant, vertical, verticillate, vertiginous, in the shade of branches even vespertine. (*HL* 7)

Obviously, this artificer goes to great lengths to accentuate the "monstrous arrogance" of constructs such as "slim, meticulous eucalyptus" and "farrago of light, colour, haze and copious air." The eucalyptus, native to Australia, is rarely slim and hardly ever meticulous. Its name derives from the Greek *"kaluptos,"* meaning "covered" because its flower hides under a cover prior to opening. "Farrago," from the Latin *"farrago,"*—a mixed fodder for cattle— also means "of immaterial things" *(OED)*. Similarly, our narrator alternately covers and reveals himself as he feeds his audience a mixed bag of literary voices and poses. The alterations in voice accentuate, not the "immateriality of things," but rather the materiality of language—the volatile, vital capabilities of words and the ways sound shapes content. The alliteration and assonance of "furze," "fir," and "further" begins to break down with "fine," but holds out long enough to author "farrago." Even more exaggerated is the "vert, verdant, vertical, verticillate, vertiginous" sequence which finally dissipates itself in "vespertine."

The passage recalls Finn MacCool's extensive mythic orations in *At Swim* where verbal emanations magically call forth related sounds. But the narrator here seems more intent on burlesquing the idea of enchantment; he presents a description with the oral emphasis of ancient incantation to sport with the reader's inclination to proceed through pages "spellbound." At the same time, O'Brien parodies the self-conscious narrator's proclivity for getting caught up in self-display. In the "vert" into "vespertine" sequence, all the adjectives except "verdant" follow each other alphabetically and appear on the same page of many dictionaries. It looks as if O'Brien wants his fiction-maker to get caught, as Myles na Gopaleen often was, consulting standard works of reference.

The passage shares essential affinities with one of Mark Twain's which exploits a compatible narrative distortion. In "A Double-Barreled Detective Story," Twain involves the reader in a ratiocinative "thriller" plot of misdirected revenge. Chapter Four then yanks the rug out with a slippery fictive feint:

> It was a crisp and spicy morning in early October. The lilacs and laburnums, lit with the glory-fires of autumn, hung burning and flashing in the upper air, a fairy bridge provided by kind Nature for the wingless wild things that have their homes in the treetops and would visit together; the larch and the pomegranate flung their purple and yellow flames in brilliant broad splashes along the slanting sweep of the woodland; the sensuous fragrance of innumerable deciduous flowers rose upon the swooning atmosphere; far in the empty sky a solitary esophagus slept upon motionless wing; everywhere brooded stillness, serenity, and the peace of God.[22]

In a series of subsequent footnotes, Twain rebukes an assortment of trusting readers who swallowed the deception whole: "I told him [a professor in a New England university] to carefully read the whole paragraph, and he would find not a vestige of sense in any detail of it."[23] Like Twain, O'Brien is "fishing for the innocent—the innocent and confiding."[24] Such angling works because we all, at times, get hooked confiding with novels.

One of the immediate pleasures of reading fiction is losing sense of oneself while sitting in a favorite chair, balancing a bound collection of words between hands. Without any conscious effort, we begin to exist within the world of the novel, innocently internalizing its sensations, images, feelings, ideas. We tend, by de-grees, to become less the reader and more a participant, existing inside its realm, living the thoughts and events of the characters as they make their way through the plot. In *The Dalkey Archive*, O'Brien periodically gives us a Twain-like shake; his narrator flaunts his function as a shaping sensibility, successfully interfer-ing with a reader's inclination toward sympathetic rapport. His intrusions jar us into recognizing that we are running our eyes over black marks on a page and—when at his best—he reminds us that these black marks refer to other ink on other leaves in other texts.

The narrator's interferences become more sporadic and subtler after the opening. We read *Dalkey* with uncertainty because the shaping sensibility often effaces himself behind a story which wants to seem, for the most part, plausible. The novel apparently revolves around the protagonist, Mick Shaughnessy, a young man finding himself and facing all the usual uninteresting complica-tions coming of age. ("What kind of work am I suited for?" and "How will Mom get on if I marry?") His many "probable" predica-ments need not be summarized, but two fantastic complications require explanation.

While going for a swim by Dalkey, Mick and his pal Hackett meet up with the eccentric philosopher and scientist De Selby. Over a glass of homemade whiskey, De Selby confides that his latest invention, DMP, will be used to destroy all life on earth by annihilating atmospheric oxygen. He also explains that in testing DMP he has made a concomitant unexpected discovery: ". . . a de-oxygenated atmosphere cancels the apparently serial nature of time and confronts us with true time and simultaneously with all the things and creatures which time has ever contained or will contain, provided we evoke them" (*DA* 22).

To subsantiate his claim, De Selby outfits Mick and Hackett with scuba equipment and leads them to an undersea chamber sealed off and airtight at high tide. He releases a small amount of DMP, annihilates the oxygen, and transforms the chamber into a zone of timelessness. The scientist then calls on St. Augustine to make an appearance and discusses theology with him for one half hour.

Two brief notes, although directly referring to *The Third Po-liceman*, provide evidence that O'Brien had been letting plot ingre-dients of "trapped time" and catastrophic annihilation ferment for over twenty years. In an holograph note found among his letters, O'Brien has Joe (the narrator's soul) explain the nature of circular, simultaneous, trapped time: "He [Joe] said it was again the beginning of the unfinished, the re-discovery of the familiar, the re-experience of the already-suffered, the fresh forgetting of the unremembered."[25] Writing to Patience Ross at Longmans Green in 1939, O'Brien interrelated his unfinished manuscript of *The Third Policeman* with the commencement of World War II—a connection which ultimately results in *The Dalkey Archive*'s associating sealed time with global destruction: "I started another story (very different indeed) about August last but gave it up owing to the threatened disintegration of the universe."[26]

Convinced that De Selby poses a real threat, Mick begins devising ways to steal the DMP and save us all. In the process, he discovers James Joyce alive and well and tending bar in Skerries. The author of "silence, exile, cunning" actually turns out to be garrulous, patriotic, and forthright. To make matters worse, he adamantly denies any connection with that piece of "pornography and filth and literary vomit," *Ulysses* (194). At the time of its composition, he was bowdlerizing great French literature for English readers. And he can prove it. Professing a lifelong ambition to join the Jesuits, Joyce succeeds in eliciting Mick's promise of assistance.

O'Brien and Niall Montgomery had many a good laugh toying with various possibilities for this Joyce subplot. While O'Brien was still composing the novel, Montgomery offered a brilliant satiric send up of authorial egotism and literary critical esoterics:

> My feeling about the J.A.J. thing is as follows. That was a man of terrifying conceit. What killed him was not ordinary illness but utter astonishment and desolation over the public failure to rave over F.W. [Finnegans Wake].
>
> If Joyce were living now there would be no happier man: I recently bought from Hodges Figgis a book twice the size of the telephone directory called A CONCORDANCE TO FINNEGANS WAKE. It lists all the words in the book and costs £ 5.0.0d! Wouldn't Mr. J. be pleased?
>
> To my ~~humble~~ mind the satire would be that Joyce since his death spent the intervening nightmare years writing "Structure & Motif in Finnegans Wake," "A First Draft Version of Finnegans Wake," "A Census of Finnegans Wake," etc., and editing from New South Wales the periodical called A WAKE NEWSLETTER, operating from Skerries under such names as Mrs. Adaline Glasheen, Hugh Kenner, Clive Hart, Fritz Zenn, Andrew Cass, David Hayman, etc. etc. founding the James Joyce Society dressed up as Paddy Column, etc.
>
> His re-action to the news of De Selby's intention of destroying the world would be indignation & dismay![27]

O'Brien's response to Montgomery rejects such open satire but highlights his focus on scoffing at "learned," limited reading procedures:

The J.A.J. development you suggest for TDA is ridiculous. Dragging him in at all is gratuitous but, I hold, defensible for the purpose of weighing down the book's message of derision. But you overlook some facts I insist on keeping in sight—(i) TDA will be read by middle-class chiners of reasonable education; (ii) about 50% of them will have HEARD the name James Joyce; (iii) about 3% will have read something BY Joyce (iv) the fraction who have read any of the exegetic bullshit or are aware of its absurdities is too tiny to be expressed.[28]

These two wild indulgences, the De Selby and Joyce episodes, coalesce surprisingly well with an ordinary, humdrum plot because the storyteller's delivery is so prosaic. The description of the mandatory girlfriend, Mary, (which recalls Brother Barnabas's description, in "Scenes in a Novel," of the "exquisite creature" Shiela) evinces our narrator's mundane behind-the-curtain manner:

Mick was absolutely sure in mind about few things but he thought he could sincerely say that Mary was an unusual girl. She was educated, with a year in France, and understood music. She had wit, could be lively, and it took little to induce for a while gaiety of word and mood. . . . She was tasteful and fastidious in dress . . . and why not? She worked in what was called a fashion house, with a top job which Mick knew paid well and involved consorting only with people of standing. (DA 58–59)

Early on, Mick meets his ladylove in Herbert Park and decides to open his mind to her. We savor the dramatic irony of Mick trying to explain the menace of De Selby and his underwater interview with St. Augustine. Of course, we know that Mick is telling the truth—we were with him when it happened. Mary, however, maintains more than a modicum of disbelief, chipping in with qualmish questions: "What's the purpose of all this bosh? Am I supposed to laugh? . . . Was a feed of whiskey the foundation of this rigmarole?" (DA 62–63). The narrator obliquely answers such questions when he breaks in with an admission of contrivance: "That account of their chat is not accurate, but it was substantially the way the queer experience was mentioned" (DA 63).

The interpretive sensibility "frames" his composition the way Algernon does a musical score in The Importance of Being Earnest.

After impressing himself with a polychromatic improvisation at the piano, Algernon informs his manservant Lane: "I don't play accurately—anyone can play accurately—but I play with wonderful expression."[29] Like Algernon, the narrator of *Dalkey* variably foresakes "accuracy" in order to play with wonderful expressions. Penetrating these expressions, an attentive reader is likely to discover that they interestingly echo other expressions of antecedent literary storytellers.

"Straight" descriptions are often laced with stock metaphors which we can recognize from other reading experiences. Chapter Nine opens with a desiccated instance of pathetic fallacy:

> The old coloured houses of irregular size along the narrow quays of the Liffey seem to lean outward as if to study themselves in the water; but on his pleasant walk there this time, Mick's eye was not dwelling pleasurably on them. He was thinking, though not in gloom. There had come to him an idea that seemed bright, masterly, bold even. (*DA* 83)

In this "simple" passage, we encounter a present tense trope which has been mined so often that the shaft is all but spent. The narrator banks on the reader remembering and juxtaposing similar images from previous fictions. Surely, those familiar with Poe recall the "vacant and eye-like windows" of Roderick Usher's house brooding over the tarn. Dickens, too, often strategically establishes the mood of an environment by referring to the houses which people it:

> Ten thousand responsible houses surrounded him [Arthur Clennam in *Little Dorrit*], frowning as heavily on the streets they composed, as if they were every one inhabited by the ten young men of the Calender's story, who blackened their faces and bemoaned their miseries every night.[30]

Closer to home is Joyce's opening to "Araby":

> North Richmond Street, being blind, was a quiet street except at the hour when the Christian Brothers' School set the boys free. An uninhabited house of two storeys stood at the blind end, detached from its neighbours in a square ground. The other houses of the street, conscious of decent lives within them, gazed at one another with brown imperturbable faces.[31]

In each of these antecedent instances—and there are certainly many more—the residential invigoration works well thematically and artistically. As we all know, Poe correlates the man and the manse; Dickens impresses an atmosphere of depression; and Joyce begins setting up motifs of blindness and isolation. In *Dalkey*, however, the narrator consciously exposes his descriptions as desiccated and inappropriate. The houses leaning over the riverbank have little to do with the story of Mick, De Selby, and Augustine. Admittedly, one could force some connection between the houses mirroring in the river and Mick "reflecting" as he walks. But we are kept from such a mistake by the narrator's self-conscious parody. He parades the pedestrian quality of an overworked set piece, reminding us that we have seen it all before.

In *At Swim*, the first-person student narrator is inclined to brandish his sense of originality by flourishing exorbitant, self-congratulating literary inventions. This narrator, however, employs the opposite tack, impressing with his deliberately designed clumsiness. Chapter Twelve opens: "The floor of that apartment in Mick's head which he liked to call the spare room was becoming a bit littered and untidy. Several tides seemed to be running simultaneously on the same shore, if that metaphor serves better" (*DA* 128). That last semiobsequious phrase is well timed, prompting a smile and assuring us that the speaker knows what he is up to. His parodies operate centrifugally—contesting these recognizable images with those of other texts—as well as centripetally—exposing the shortcomings of established narrative procedures.

Because Joyce is creatively ransomed as a character in this novel, we are immediately reminded of similar configurations in *Dubliners* and *A Portrait*. In "Araby," the young boy begins to treasure the make-believe when he discovers *The Abbot*, *The Devout Communicant*, and *The Memoirs of Vidocq*. in "the waste room behind the kitchen . . . littered with old useless papers."[32] Set against this apartment, housing a small but fertile literary heritage, the "spare room" in Mick's head proves barren indeed. The second metaphor, "several tides seemed to be running simultaneously on the same shore," evokes the variety of currents which lap at Stephen Dedalus, especially the springtide of sordidness which overwhelms Stephen's regime:

> How foolish his aim had been! He had tried to build a breakwater of order and elegance against the sordid tide of life without him and to dam up, by rules of conduct and active interests and new filial relations, the powerful recurrence of the tides within him.[33]

Mick Shaughnessy will develop similar redemptive regimes, but for now it is enough to establish that *Dalkey*'s tidal metaphors mingle with those of *A Portrait* and deliberately do not "serve better."

O'Brien's narrator frequently composes passages which shrewdly rub elbows with characters, images, and novelistic patterns which have gone before. While pretending to go with the flow of straightforward fiction, he sometimes slips in a subtle undertow. The title itself inclines in this direction. When Mick first discovers Joyce filling glasses in a Skerries pub, he leans across the bar and tells him: "It is a really deep pleasure to meet a man of your attainments face to face. Your name stands high in the world. You are a most remarkable writer, an innovator, Dublin's incomparable archivist" (*DA* 144). Joyce is "Dublin's incomparable archivist" because he took a city's topography and its citizens' type of talk and created a new institution—the "Dublin" authorized by his short stories and novels. For O'Brien to call his little spoof *The Dalkey Archive* is to posture that he is doing for Dalkey what Joyce did for Dublin. The wry incongruities are consistent with the backhanded nature of the book.

Dalkey abounds with funny talk by the characters, but the undersea interview with St. Augustine proves the most provocative of the comic conversations. All of the "redemptions" which Mick Shaughnessy will try to effect later in the novel are satirically discredited long before their genesis. In a cavern cut off from "reality" by high tide, De Selby and the Bishop of Hippo engage each other in a Collopy-Fahrt set of "learned" exchanges. The experiment is supposedly undertaken in the interest of science; however, De Selby probes with the most ludicrous questions:

> Were all your rutting ceremonials heterosexual? . . .
> Did you suffer from haemorrhoids? . . .
> Would it be seemly to call you callous humbug? . . .
> Are you a Nigger? (*DA* 36, 41, 40, 44)

Although an esteemed philosopher and a Father of the Church, Augustine returns serve blasphemously, exploding the Christian traditions he supposedly solidified. He uses the occasion of the theological disputation to abuse the most revered figures in the Bible. According to Augustine, the holy saints Peter and Paul seem to spend most of their time in heaven dodging desecratious barbs:

> Peter's just out to show off the keys, bluster about and make himself a bloody nuisance. . . . The lads in our place, when he barges around encorpified and flashing the keys, can't resist taking a rise out of him and pursue him with the cackles of a rooster, cockadoodle-doo. . . .

Paul is in our place, often encorpified and always attended by his physician Luke, putting poultices on his patient's sore neck. When Paul shows too much consate in himself, the great blatherskite with his epistles in bad Greek, the chronic two-timer, I sometimes roar after him "You're not on the road to Damascus now!" Puts him in his place. (*DA* 38–40)

The roasting also includes the major "critics" of the Bible, those translators and experts in exegesis who have so influenced the shape of various subsequent texts. One of the early Fathers of the Church, Origen of Alexandria, is traditionally revered for his heroic response to the occasion of sin. Augustine refers to him as "that ante-Nicene thooleramawn" and presents his own version of the religious sacrifice:

What did he do when he found that lusting after women distracted him from his sacred scrivenery? I'll tell you. He stood up, hurried out to the kitchen, grabbed a carving knife and—pwitch!—in one swipe deprived himself of his personality! Ah? . . .
How could Origen be the Father of Anything and he with no knackers on him? (*DA* 37)

Augustine discredits his own infamous "Fatherhood" by lampooning his celebrated redemptive conversion, frankly admitting to making up the stuff as he went along. His revered *Confessions* dramatizes the transformation of a pagan hedonist into an enlightened defender of the Catholic faith. However, Augustine spotlights the fictionality of his local-boy-makes-good text; he denies the libertine excursions for which his *Confessions* are most remembered:

I invented obscene feats out of bravado, lest I be thought innocent or cowardly. I walked the streets of Babylon with low companions, sweating from the fires of lust. When I was in Carthage I carried about with me a cauldron of unrealised debauchery. God in his majesty was tempting me. But Book Two of my *Confessions* is all shocking exaggeration. I lived within my rough time. And I kept the faith, unlike a lot more of my people in Algeria who are now Arab nincompoops and slaves of Islam. (*DA* 36–37)

References to Augustine's famous "*Tolle Lege*" incident further dissipate all the motifs of redemption. In perhaps the most curious case of reader response, Augustine is supposedly converted when he obeys a heavenly voice calling "*Tolle Lege, Tolle Lege*"— take up and read. Opening the first book which catches his eye (to the right page), he is saved by apostolic exhortations to follow Jesus:

> The first book I picked up was by Paul and the lines that struck my eyes were these: "Not in rioting or drunkenness, nor in chambering or wantonness, nor in strife or envying: but put ye on the Lord Jesus Christ and make not provision for the flesh in the lusts thereof." But do you know, I think the greatest dog's breakfast of the lot is St. Vianney. . . . the curé of Ars. . . . ignorant as the back of a cab. (*DA* 40–41)

Although Augustine claims that the experience was "no conjuring trick," he belies the miracle by admitting to tall tales, vilifying Paul, and packaging it all in well-worn Dublinese wrapping.

The Dublin pub accent in the mouth of a Mediterranean not only confirms the religious ridicule, it also inclines the plot of Mick and his problems toward parody. O'Brien obviously takes perverse pleasure in violating the tenets and traditions of the Bible—the holier the scripture the more urgent the transgression. Probably more than any other text, the Bible has shaped the imaginative framework of western man. As William Blake declares, "The Old and the New Testaments are the Great Code of Art." The typologies, symbols, and myths from Genesis through Apocalypse clearly inform a great deal of our cultural inheritance including—or perhaps especially—literature. One of the fundamental religious tropes accommodated by the classical novel is the provision of redemption. Secularized in the *bildungsroman*, the young protagonist redeems a self as he either rejects or joins the adult communal world to which he has felt foreign. In a manner similar to *At Swim*, *The Dalkey Archive* willfully trespasses in this field by placing Mick's quest for redemption alongside those of Augustine and Stephen Dedalus.

Like Joyce's "hero," Mick's coming of age entails constructing several breakwaters to redirect and dam the sordid tides of life without and within. First, he resolves to abstain from alcohol, substituting salubrious Vichy water for porter and whiskey. This transformation, he believes, is a necessary prerequisite if he is "to do something" to thwart De Selby. Unlike Origen of Alexandria, however, Mick feels capable of looking temptation in the eye: "He was pleased. He resolved to go to a quiet place where alcoholic drinks were to be had and then, please God, not have one but try something healthy, refreshing, harmless. Plain thinking—planning—was called for" (*DA* 83).

Like Stephen with his prize money, Mick consolidates his fi-

THE CRAFT OF SEEMING PEDESTRIAN

nances, opens a checking account, and takes a *Portrait*-like plea-sure in his stature as agent of arrangement: "Thus for some days his life was quiet, almost decorous. He thought a bit about his growing, if secret, importance in the world he walked, his quiet command of the issues in a confrontation that was quite fabulous" (*DA* 102).

Mick relishes each new complication of plot as an opportunity to affirm himself as author of order. Each new thread, like the discovery of James Joyce in Skerries, can be interlaced into the web he thinks he weaves. Stephen Dedalus often attempts to assert control through the act of writing. On the flyleaf of his geography he composes "himself" within a hierarchy of spatial place; after winning his prize money, he draws up "a form of commonwealth for the household"; determined to record his flight, he forges in his diary "the subject of my revolt."[34] Mick Shaughnessy, however, can do Stephen one better; he has no need to write things down. He can pare his fingernails as he mentally constructs a detailed nine-point plan which will not only preserve mankind, but will redeem the Redeemer. Excerpts from this ingenous scheme should provide a flavor of its grandeur:

1. De Selby's cask had to be stolen as soon as possible with the co-operation of Sergeant Fottrell.
2. To the end of (1) he would make a bogus appointment with De Selby at the Colza Hotel and, by pre-arrangement with Hackett, have him detained there while he, Mick, and the Sergeant rifled his house.
3. To the end of (2) he would have to . . .
4. He would have to devise, . . .
6. Assuming he met Joyce and won his confidence, could the con-tretemps at (4) be resolved by . . .
7. . . . his present situation was that he was on the point of rescuing everybody from obliteration, somewhat as it was claimed that Jesus had redeemed all mankind. Was he not himself a god-figure of some sort?
8. . . . If he now carried out successfully his plan to rescue all God's creatures, was there not a sort of concomitant obligation . . . to save the Almighty as well as his terrestrial brood . . .?
9. . . . was it his duty to overturn the Holy Father himself? (*DA* 128–29)

Swept up in the surge of his "personal majesty," Mick feels obliged to break off his relationship with Mary. Ironically, the great arranger is still the slave of cliché: "He had, so to speak, no use for her washing" (*DA* 187). Mick postulates that his godlike redemptive tasks will probably take up all his time, requiring a celibate existence: "He was supervising men of indeterminate calibre, of sanity that was more than suspect. Clearly enough this task had been assigned to him by Almighty God, and this gave him somewhat the status of priest." (*DA* 156).

Like Stephen in his intermediate phase, Mick thinks he hears the call of a religious vocation. His great "vision" here, his "epiphany" of election, is repeatedly phrased to summon parodic comparisons with Stephen's climax on the strand when he imagines himself as "the great artificer."[35] Mick's soaring insight takes place, not on the beach, but in the middle of St. Stephen's Green, which the narrator takes great care to describe with the fatuous diction, tone, rhythms of a travel brochure:

> The Green is a railed-in square pleasure ground near the city centre, an extravagance of flower beds and fountains. A pretty lake, spanned at the centre by a bridge and having little islands, was the home of water fowl, many exotic and matching the flowers in hue and life. . . . He [Mick] leaned back, closed his eyes, and meditated. . . . He rather admired his own adroit manipulation of matters which, in certain regards, transcended this world. (*DA* 151)

Some of his "meditations" closely resemble Stephen's: "His mood was a formless one of renunciation. What about his mother?" (*DA* 156). Yet eventually, his mental ecstasies of flight digress into bizarre inanities: "To say there is a time and a place for everything is trite, but the truth of the sentiment is not to be denied for all that; one could play the accordion while having a bath but probably nobody has ever tried to do that" (*DA* 157).

Fortunately, Mick's highflying hopes are definitively grounded. The novel concludes quickly, with Mick meeting Mary and Hackett in the lounge of the Colza hotel, intent on announcing "the redemption of his soul" (*DA* 216). The "careful, conclusive foray in his life" turns instead into a rout of pathetic reconciliation. In a matter of minutes, he falls off the wagon, proposes to Mary, and is relegated to raising future progeny generated without his creative efforts. The narrator quickly and aptly dismisses the whole affair: "That is as much as need be told. The silence between them on the home-bound tram was mutually known and nursed. What had happened, after all? Nothing much" (*DA* 222).

Making much of nothing, O'Brien offhandedly discloses his flair for extending his fictions by working with and off the words of others. With subdued sport, he scoffingly emulates the disposition of novels to revolve around character, determining predictable paths through spent serial arrangements. Early in his career,

O'Brien's tenor was openly ostentatious. *At Swim's* multiple openings, exaggerated fragmentations, and Chinese-box puzzles forcibly explode the formulations we are used to finding and making in novels. By the end of his career, however, O'Brien is underplaying his performance. By spuriously conforming to conventional formats, *The Dalkey Archive* powerfully implodes continuity, developments, and redemption. Instead of pushing through the boundaries of fiction, this novel yanks them out of shape through its gravitational parody.

Writing to his publisher, Timothy O'Keeffe, O'Brien said of his last complete novel: "The book is not meant to be a novel or anything of the kind but a study in derision, various writers with their styles, and sundry modes, attitudes and cults being the rats in the cage."[36] By "not a novel" O'Brien means that his book merely feigns a realistic approach. As a textual experiment, *The Dalkey Archive* entails letting the rats out of their cages and making them sing for their supper. The real master of revels is not De Selby, but O'Brien's elusive third-person narrator. Alternatively headlining and hiding behind his props, he triumphantly directs the production as "no less than comic-opera subterfuge" (*DA* 151).

Notes

Chapter 1. *Comhthrom Feinne* and *Blather:* The Early Experiments

1. John D. MacDonald, *The Dreadful Lemon Sky* (New York: Fawcett, 1974), 205.

2. To date, the fullest (but still incomplete) collection of O'Brien's *Comhthrom Feinne* and *Blather* articles is *Myles Before Myles,* with an introduction by John Wyse Jackson (London: Grafton, 1988).

3. Flann O'Brien (Brian O'Nolan), *Comhthrom Feinne* (Dublin, 1931–1935), I.2.31–32. All further references will be cited in the text by volume, number, and page numbers with the abbreviation *CF.*

4. Niall Montgomery, "An Aristophanic Sorcerer," *Irish Times,* 2 April 1966.

5. Flann O'Brien (Brian O'Nolan), *Blather* (Dublin, 1934–1935), I.5.92 and I.1.3. All further references will be cited in the text by volume, number, and page numbers with the abbreviation *B.*

6. Flann O'Brien (Brian O'Nolan), *The Third Policeman* (1967; reprinted New York: NAL, 1976), 56–57. All further references will be cited in the text with the abbreviation *TP.*

7. Flann O'Brien (Brian O'Nolan), *The Best of Myles* (1968; reprinted London: Pan, 1975), 101–2.

8. Flann O'Brien (Brian O'Nolan), *At Swim-Two-Birds* (1939; reprinted New York: NAL, 1966), 142. All further references will be cited in the text with the abbreviation *AS.*

9. Anne Clissmann, *Flann O'Brien: A Critical Introduction to His Writings* (Dublin: Gill and Macmillan; New York: Barnes, 1975), 40–41.

10. Ibid., 43.

11. James Joyce, *A Portrait of the Artist as a Young Man* (1916; reprinted New York: Penguin, 1980), 215.

12. Ibid.

13. Sean Kilfeather of the *Irish Times* sports department has generously assisted me in identifying some of the phrases. Many are familiar to any American who grew up with "ABC's Wide World of Sports," but some are obscure enough to baffle even dedicated disciples of *The Sporting News.* This abbreviated reference guide should help the reader follow The O'Blather as he expeditiously changes uniforms:

Scrum = rugby.

Queen's Gambit, pawns, etc. = chess.

Five sets = tennis.

Safe pair of hands, etc. = Gaelic football. The wording refers to the ability to catch the ball cleanly and kick it a long distance.

Cue ball, double-baulk, pots, long jenny = billards (in part, snooker).

Half-time score = bowls (and possibly cricket) "Rec. 1000" suggests that the match is handicapped with Belgium receiving 1000 points to start.
Slow bowler, pitch, cover point, silly-mid-on = cricket.
Stumps were drawn = umpires pulling up the wicket to signify that the match is over.
Three strokes in hand, half the sixteenth, irons = golf.
Handling movement, try = rugby again.
Solid = a winning or decisive score in handball.

14. After the final issue of *Blather*, January 1935, O'Brien occasionally wrote for *Comhthrom Feinne* again. Many of the *At Swim* impulses are evident in the articles "What's Wrong with the 'L and H'" (X.3.58–59), and "Tidying the Garden" (XI.2.36–37). In these, he castigates bores, demonstrates an acute awareness of audience, and urges the advantages of "destructive sanity."

15. O'Brien liked this material so much that he "borrowed" it for the first issue of *Blather*. He crossed this piece with another Brother Barnabas essay, "Should Pin-Money Girls Be Sacked?: Mein Kampf" (*CF* VI.3.47–48), to arrive at a hybrid which announced the birth of The O'Blather.

Chapter 2. *At Swim-Two-Birds:* Exorbitance and the Early Manuscripts

1. Clissmann, *Critical Introduction*, xiii.

2. Two manuscript versions of the novel are housed at the Harry Ransom Humanities Research Center, The University of Texas at Austin. The earlier version *(MS1)* is an amalgam of at least two typescripts with hundreds of autograph additions and emendations. The opening jottings and last eleven pages are entirely holograph. The exact dates of composition are unknown, but the manuscript was most likely composed between 1934 and 1937. *MS1* was purchased by HRHRC from Bertram Rota Ltd., London, in 1970. The later manuscript version of the novel *(MS2)* is, according to O'Brien, a carbon copy of the final typescript submitted to Longmans Green in 1938. *MS2* was purchased by HRHRC from Frank Hollings, London, in 1962.

3. I. A. Richards, *Principles of Literary Criticism* (New York: Harcourt, 1928), 240.

4. David Hume, *An Abstract of a Treatise of Human Nature*, ed. J. M. Keynes and P. Sraffa (Hamden, Conn.: Archon, 1965), 11–12.

5. O'Brien to Mannin, 10 July 1939, Brian O'Nolan Collection, Morris Library, Southern Illinois University, Carbondale, Illinois. All letters cited are from this collection.

6. Richard Chase, *The American Novel and Its Traditions* (New York: Gordian, 1957), ix.

7. Patricia Tobin, *Time and the Novel* (Princeton: Princeton University Press, 1978), 6.

8. Edward Said, *Beginnings: Intention and Method* (New York: Basic Books, 1975), 82.

9. Denis Donoghue, "French Structuralist Theories," *Partisan Review*, no. 3 (1980):399.

10. Michel Foucault, *The Archaeology of Knowledge*, tr. A. M. Sheridan Smith (New York: Harper, 1976), 169.

11. Laurence Sterne, *Tristram Shandy* (1759–67; reprinted Boston: Houghton, 1959), 43.

12. Henry James, *The Art of the Novel* (New York: Scribners, 1974), 33.

13. In 1905, Percival Lowell posited the existence of a ninth planet using the same procedures to account for the exorbitance of Neptune. With the aid of his calculations, Pluto was officially discovered in 1930. Currently, the exorbitant behavior of Pluto has led to speculations about a tenth planet in our solar system, hypothetically labeled "Planet X."

14. José Ortega y Gasset, "Notes on the Novel," in *The Dehumanization of Art* (Princeton: Princeton University Press, 1948), 98–99, 103.

15. Ibid., 79.

16. See, for example, Clissmann, *Critical Introduction*, 82.

17. John Wain, "To Write for My Own Race," *Encounter* (July 1967):71.

18. Aldoux Huxley, *Point Counter Point* (1928; reprinted New York: Harper, 1965), 301–2.

19. Edgar Allan Poe, "William Wilson," in *Edgar Allan Poe: Selected Prose Poetry and Eureka*, ed. W. H. Auden (New York: Harper, 1950), 42.

20. Foucault, *Archaeology*, 207.

21. J. Hillis Miller, "Three Problems of Fictional Form," in *Experience and the Novel*, ed. Roy Harvey Pierce (New York: Columbia University Press, 1968), 92.

22. Ortega y Gasset, "Notes on the Novel," 91–92.

23. Clissmann, *Critical Introduction*, 148.

24. Ruth ApRoberts, "*At Swim-Two-Birds* and the Novel as Self-Evident Sham," *Eire-Ireland* 6, no. 2 (summer 1971):87, 96.

25. Ibid., 97.

26. Rudiger Imhof, *Alive Alive O!: Flann O'Brien's At Swim-Two-Birds* (Dublin: Wolfhound; New York: Barnes, 1985), 15.

27. Miller, "Three Problems," 27.

28. Frank Kermode, *The Sense of an Ending* (New York: Oxford University Press, 1967), 18.

Chapter 3. *At Swim-Two-Birds:* Verbal Gamesmanship and Palimpsest

1. In *MS1* O'Brien changed "a plurality of openings" and "twenty-seven endings" to "three different openings and twenty seven endings or twenty-two times that number . . ." prior to settling on the final version in the novel (*MS1* 1).

2. Robert Frost, ". . . the beginning of a book's career," in *Robert Frost: Poetry and Prose*, ed. Edward C. Lathem and Lawrance Thompson (New York: Henry Holt, 1972), 253, 251.

3. George Puttenham, *The Arte of English Poesie*, ed. Gladys Doidge Willcock et al (London: Cambridge University Press, 1936), 184.

4. This terminology is derived from Terence Hawkes's *Structuralism and Semiotics* (Berkeley: University of California Press, 1977).

5. Vivian Mercier, *The Irish Comic Tradition* (London: Oxford University Press, 1962), 97–98.

6. Flann O'Brien (Brian O'Nolan), "George Bernard Shaw on Language," *Irish Times*, 23 January 1965.

7. Richards, *Principles of Literary Criticism*, 240.

8. Maurice Evans, "Introduction," in *The Countess of Pembroke's Arcadia*, by Sir

Philip Sidney (New York: Penguin, 1977), 14.

9. John Hoskins, *Directions for Speech and Style*, ed. Hoyt H. Hudson (Princeton: Princeton University Press, 1935), 46.

10. Ibid., 47.

11. Evans, "Introduction," 15.

12. Thomas Kinsella, ed. and trans., *The Tain* (London: Oxford University Press, 1975), xiv.

13. Ibid., 250.

14. Hawkes, *Structuralism and Semiotics*, 62.

15. Ibid.

16. V. S. Pritchett, "Death of Finn," *New Statesman* 60 (20 August 1960), 250.

17. Ibid.

18. Gerard Murphy, *The Ossianic Lore and Romantic Tales of Medieval Ireland* (Dublin: Three Candles, 1961), 16.

19. Ibid., 19.

20. Flann O'Brien (Brian O'Nolan), "Standish Hayes O'Grady," *Irish Times*, 16 October 1940.

21. Standish Hayes O'Grady, *Silva Gadelica* (1892; reprinted New York: Lemma, 1970), 100.

22. O'Grady explains that he used the Egerton MS in the British Museum, written in 1780–82 by Maurice O'Connor who probably transcribed from a copy (now in the Royal Irish Academy) made by his tutor John Murphy. O'Brien probably encountered the Murphy MS while researching his master's thesis in the Royal Irish Academy. See Ibid., vi and ix.

23. Mercier, *The Irish Comic Tradition*, 6.

24. Rubin Flower, *The Irish Tradition* (Oxford: Clarendon, 1974), 105.

25. Mercier, *The Irish Comic Tradition*, 8.

26. Thomas Pynchon, *The Crying of Lot 49* (1966; reprinted New York: Bantam, 1972), 103–4.

27. J. G. O'Keeffe, *The Adventures of Suibhne Geilt* (London: The Irish Texts, 1913), x.

28. See Ibid., xiii–iv, for a description of the manuscripts he used. Two were available to O'Brien in the Royal Irish Academy. O'Brien told Longmans that he performed his own translations of *Buile Suibhne*.

29. Ibid., 13.

30. Karl Miller, "Gael in Wonderland," *New York Review of Books* (1 May 1965), 30.

31. J. C. C. Mays, "Brian O'Nolan: Literalist of the Imagination," in *Myles: Portraits of Brian O'Nolan*, ed. Timothy O'Keeffe (London: Martin Brian, 1973), 87.

32. apRoberts, "Self-Evident Sham," 90–91.

33. Willi Apel et al., *The Harvard Brief Dictionary of Music* (New York: Pocket Books, 1974), 19.

34. Mays, "Brian O'Nolan," 87.

35. Robert Frost, "On Extravagance," in *Robert Frost: Poetry and Prose*, ed. Edward C. Lathem and Lawrance Thompson (New York: Holt, 1972), 449.

36. Samuel Beckett, *Murphy* (1938; reprinted New York: Grove, 1957), 40.

37. Lillian Hellman, *Pentimento* (New York: NAL, 1973), 3.

38. The idea of a comic stripper is nothing new but the ingenuity of applying the routine to O'Brien's novel belongs to Holly Beth King. She has allowed me to read her unpublished essay "A Particularly Irish Stew: Flann O'Brien and *At Swim-Two-Birds*," and to appropriate the metaphor so that I might creatively deform it.

Chapter 4. *The Third Policeman:* "Re-Inscribing" the Self

1. If the fan's speed is a multiple or simple fraction of sixty revolutions per second, the blades will also appear to be standing still. See "Science Times," *The New York Times* (3 August 1982):C2.

2. Hume, *Human Nature*, 11, 14–15.

3. Charles Maturin, *Melmoth the Wanderer* (London: Oxford University Press, 1968), 187.

4. Clissmann, *Critical Introduction*, 156, 175.

5. By an interesting coincidence, *The Wizard of Oz* premiered in 1939, the same year O'Brien was composing *The Third Policeman*.

6. Joseph Conrad, *Heart of Darkness* (1902; reprinted New York: Bantam, 1969), 44.

7. Sigmund Freud, *The Interpretation of Dreams*, trans. and ed. James Strachey (London: Hogarth, 1964), 588.

8. This house, the light, and the tree closely resemble the stage setting for W. B. Yeats's play *Purgatory* (also 1939). Although Yeats's play and O'Brien's novel differ thematically, they share a similar strange "big house" as well as a focus on disturbing, circular repetitions.

9. James Merrill, "Condemned to Write about Things Real," *New York Times Book Review* (21 February 1982):11.

10. I am indebted to Edward Said's explanation of Michel Foucault's ideal historian. See his "An Ethics of Language," *Diacritics*, 4, no. 2 (1974):30.

11. Frost, "On Extravagance," 449.

12. Said, *Beginnings*, 94.

13. R. P. Blackmur, "Examples of Wallace Stevens," in *The Double Agent* (1935; reprinted Gloucester, Mass.: P. Smith, 1962), 74.

14. Pynchon, *The Crying of Lot 49*, 95.

15. This type of pseudocritical quarreling is quite similar to the *Irish Times* controversy begun by O'Brien between December 1938 and January 1939. Frank O'Connor's play *Time's Pocket* was panned by a reviewer in the *Irish Times*. Sean O'Faolain came to the rescue writing a favorable defense. O'Brien, with the help of Niall Sheridan, continued the debate for months by taking either side on alternate days (employing multiple pseudonyms) and supplying pro and con critical essays. The "literary" debate increased the readership of the newspaper remarkably and eventually led to the editor, R.M. Smyllie, hiring O'Brien to write his "Cruiskeen Lawn" column.

Chapter 5. *The Hard Life* and *The Dalkey Archive:* The Craft of Seeming Pedestrian

1. See, for example, Anthony Burgess, "Mister-piece," *Yorkshire Post*, 16 November 1961, and W. L. Webb, "Flann O'Brien's Misterpiece," *Manchester Guardian*, 17 November 1961.

2. See, for example, Clissmann, *Critical Introduction*, 271–72, and Wain, "To Write," 79–85.

3. O'Nolan to O'Keeffe, 7 June 1961.

4. Sheridan to O'Nolan, no date, labeled "Saturday," probably fall 1960.

5. O'Nolan to Heath, 20 February 1961.

6. Clissmann, *Critical Introduction*, 287.

7. Flann O'Brien (Brian O'Nolan), *The Hard Life* (1961; reprinted New York: Penguin, 1977), All further references will be cited in the text with the abbreviation *HL*.

8. O'Brien, *The Best of Myles*, 234.

9. O'Nolan to Heath, December 1960.

10. Clissmann, *Critical Introduction*, 273.

11. O'Nolan to Heath, December 1960.

12. James Joyce, *Ulysses* (New York: Random House, 1961), 162.

13. Sheridan to O'Nolan, no date, labeled "Saturday," probably fall 1960.

14. Patrick McGinley, *Bogmail* (New York: Penguin, 1982), 182.

15. O'Nolan to O'Keeffe, 27 November 1963.

16. O'Nolan to Heath, 6 January 1964.

17. O'Nolan to Montgomery, 6 January 1964.

18. Autograph response from Montgomery to O'Nolan written on the previous letter cited in note 17.

19. Flann O'Brien (Brian O'Nolan), *The Dalkey Archive* (1964; reprinted New York: Penguin, 1977), All further references will be cited in the text with the abbreviation *DA*.

20. William Shakespeare, *A Midsummer Night's Dream*, ed. Wolfgang Clemen, (New York: Signet/Penguin, 1963), I.1.147–48.

21. *The Holy Bible:* Old and New Testaments in the King James Version (Nashville: Thomas Nelson, 1976) Luke, 2.10.

22. Mark Twain (Samuel Langhorne Clemens), "A Double-Barreled Detective Story," in *The Writings of Mark Twain* (Hartford, Conn.: American Publication Company, 1903), 436.

23. Ibid., 438.

24. Ibid., 436.

25. O'Brien, holograph note to self, "Joe had been . . .", #296, O'Nolan Collection.

26. O'Nolan to Ross, 10 October 1939.

27. Autograph response from Montgomery to O'Nolan. See letter from O'Nolan to Montgomery, 6 January 1964.

28. O'Nolan to Montgomery, 10 January 1964.

29. Oscar Wilde, *The Importance of Being Earnest* (1899; reprinted New York: Avon, 1965), 27.

30. Charles Dickens, *Little Dorrit* (1857; reprinted New York: Penguin, 1967), 68.

31. James Joyce, "Araby," in *Dubliners. The Portable James Joyce* (1947; reprinted New York: Penguin, 1976), 37.

32. Ibid. 39.

33. Joyce, *A Portrait*, 98.

34. Ibid. 15–16, 97, 248.

35. Ibid. 170.

36. O'Nolan to O'Keeffe, 15 November 1963.

Select Bibliography

Apel, Willi, et al. *The Harvard Brief Dictionary of Music*. New York: Pocket Books, 1974.

Asbee, Sue. *Flann O'Brien*. Boston: Twayne, 1991.

Beckett, Samuel. *Murphy*. 1938. Reprint. New York: Grove, 1957.

Blackmur, R. P. "Examples of Wallace Stevens." In *The Double Agent*, 68–102. 1935. Reprint. Gloucester, Mass.: P. Smith, 1962.

Burgess, Anthony. "Mister-piece." (Review of *The Hard Life*, by Flann O'Brien.) *Yorkshire Post*, 16 November 1961.

Chase, Richard. *The American Novel and Its Traditions*. New York: Gordian, 1957.

Clissmann, Anne. *Flann O'Brien: A Critical Introduction to His Writings*. Dublin: Gill and Macmillan; New York: Barnes, 1975.

Conrad, Joseph. *Heart of Darkness*. 1902. Reprint. New York: Bantam, 1969.

Cronin, Anthony. *No Laughing Matter: The Life and Times of Flann O'Brien*. London: Grafton, 1989.

Dickens, Charles. *Little Dorrit*. 1857. Reprint. New York: Penguin, 1967.

Donoghue, Denis. "French Structuralist Theories." In *Partisan Review*, no. 3 (1980): 397–409.

Evans, Maurice. "Introduction" in *The Countess of Pembroke's Arcadia*, by Sir Philip Sidney. New York: Penguin, 1977.

Flower, Robin. *The Irish Tradition*. Oxford: Clarendon, 1947.

Foucault, Michel. *The Archaeology of Knowledge*. Translated by A. M. Sheridan Smith. New York: Harper, 1976.

Freud, Sigmund. *The Interpretation of Dreams*. Translated and edited by James Strachey. London: Hogarth, 1964.

Frost, Robert. ". . . the beginning of a book's career." In *Robert Frost: Poetry and Prose*. Edited by Edward C. Lathem and Lawrance Thompson, 244–57. New York: Holt, 1972.

———. "On Extravagance." In *Robert Frost: Poetry and Prose*. Edited by Edward C. Lathem and Lawrance Thompson, 447–59. New York: Holt, 1972.

Hawkes, Terence. *Structuralism and Semiotics*. Berkeley: University of California Press, 1977.

Hellman, Lillian. *Pentimento*. New York: NAL, 1973.

Holy Bible, The: Old and New Testaments in the King James Version. Nashville: Thomas Nelson, 1976.

Hoskins, John. *Directions for Speech and Style*. Edited by Hoyt H. Hudson. Princeton: Princeton University Press, 1935.

Hume, David. *An Abstract of a Treatise of Human Nature*. Edited by J. M. Keynes and P. Sraffa. Hamden, Conn.: Archon, 1965.

Huxley, Aldous. *Point Counter Point.* 1928. Reprint. New York: Harper, 1965.

Imhof, Rudiger, ed. *Alive Alive O!: Flann O'Brien's At Swim-Two-Birds.* Dublin: Wolfhound; New York: Barnes, 1985.

James, Henry. *The Art of the Novel.* New York: Scribners, 1934.

Joyce, James. "Araby." In *Dubliners. The Portable James Joyce,* 39–46. 1947. Reprint. New York: Penguin, 1976.

————. *A Portrait of the Artist as a Young Man.* 1916. Reprint. New York: Penguin, 1980.

————. *Ulysses.* New York: Random House, 1961.

Kermode, Frank. *The Sense of an Ending.* New York: Oxford University Press, 1967.

King, Holly Beth. "A Particularly Irish Stew: Flann O'Brien and *At Swim-Two-Birds.*" Typescript.

Kinsella, Thomas, ed. and trans. *The Tain.* London: Oxford University Press 1975.

MacDonald, John D. *The Dreadful Lemon Sky.* New York: Fawcett, 1974.

Maturin, Charles. *Melmoth the Wanderer.* 1820. Reprint. London: Oxford University Press, 1968.

Mays, J. C. C. "Brian O'Nolan: Literalist of the Imagination." In *Myles: Portraits of Brian O'Nolan.* Edited by Timothy O'Keeffe. London: Martin Brian, 1973.

McGinley, Patrick. *Bogmail.* New York: Penguin, 1982.

Mercier, Vivian. *The Irish Comic Tradition.* London: Oxford University Press, 1962.

Merrill, James. "Condemned to Write About Things Real." *New York Times Book Review,* 21 February 1982, 11.

Miller, J. Hillis. "Three Problems of Fictional Form." In *Experience and the Novel.* Edited by Roy Harvey Pierce. New York: Columbia University Press, 1968.

Miller, Karl. "Gael in Wonderland." *New York Review of Books,* 1 May 1965.

Montgomery, Niall. "An Aristophanic Sorcerer." *Irish Times,* 2 April 1966.

Murphy, Gerard. *The Ossianic Lore and Romantic Tales of Medieval Ireland.* Dublin: Three Candles, 1961.

O'Brien, Flann [Brian O'Nolan]. *At Swim-Two-Birds.* 1939. Reprint. New York: NAL, 1966.

————. "At Swim-Two-Birds." *MS1* and *MS2.* The Harry Ransom Humanities Research Center, University of Texas, Austin, Texas.

————. *The Best of Myles.* 1968. Reprint. London: Pan, 1975.

————. *Blather.* Dublin: I.1–I.5, August 1934–January 1935.

————. *Comhthrom Feinne.* Dublin: I.1–XI.2, May 1931–May 1935.

————. *The Dalkey Archive.* 1964. Reprint. New York: Penguin, 1977.

————. *Further Cuttings from Cruskeen Lawn.* Edited by Kevin O'Nolan. London: Hart-Davis, 1976.

————. "George Bernard Shaw On Language." *Irish Times,* 23 January 1965.

————. *The Hair of the Dogma.* Edited by Kevin O'Nolan. London: Hart-Davis, 1977.

————. *The Hard Life.* 1961. Reprint. New York: Penguin, 1977.

————. Letters to and from Brian O'Nolan. O'Nolan Collection, Morris Library, Southern Illinois University, Carbondale, Ill.

————. *Myles Before Myles*. Introduction by John Wyse Jackson. London: Grafton, 1988.

————. *The Poor Mouth* [*An Béal Bocht*]. Translated by Patrick Power. London: Hart-Davis, 1973.

————. "Standish Hayes O'Grady." *Irish Times*, 16 October 1940.

————. *The Third Policeman*. 1967. Reprint. New York: NAL, 1976.

O'Grady, Standish Hayes. *Silva Gadelica*. 1892. Reprint. New York: Lemma, 1970.

O'Keeffe, J. G. *The Adventures of Suibhne Geilt*. London: The Irish Texts, 1913.

Ortega y Gasset, José. "Notes on the Novel." In *The Dehumanization of Art*, 55–103. Princeton: Princeton University Press, 1948.

Poe, Edgar Allan. "William Wilson." In *Edgar Allan Poe: Selected Prose Poetry and Eureka*. Edited by W. H. Auden, 39–60. New York: Harper, 1950.

Pritchett, V. S. "Death of Finn." *New Statesman* 60 (20 August 1960): 250–51.

Puttenham, George. *The Arte of English Poesie*. Edited by Gladys Doidge Willcock et al. London: Cambridge University Press, 1936.

Pynchon, Thomas. *The Crying of Lot 49*. 1966. Reprint. New York: Bantam, 1972.

apRoberts, Ruth. "*At Swim-Two-Birds* and The Novel as Self-Evident Sham." *Eire-Ireland* 6, no. 2 (summer 1971): 76–97.

Richards, I. A. *Principles of Literary Criticism*. New York: Harcourt, 1928.

Said, Edward. *Beginnings: Intention and Method*. New York: Basic Books, 1975.

————. "An Ethics of Language," *Diacritics* 4, no. 2 (1974): 28–37.

Saussure, Ferdinand. *Course in General Linguistics*. Translated by Wade Baskin. New York: Harcourt, 1959.

"Science Times," *The New York Times* (3 August 1982): C2.

Shakespeare, William. *A Midsummer Night's Dream*. Edited by Wolfgang Clemen. New York: Signet/Penguin, 1963.

Sterne, Laurence. *Tristram Shandy*. 1759–67. Reprint. Boston: Houghton, 1965.

Tobin, Patricia. *Time and the Novel*. Princeton: Princeton University Press, 1978.

Twain, Mark [Samuel Langhorne Clemens]. "A Double-Barreled Detective Story." In *The Writings of Mark Twain*. Hartford, Conn.: The American Publication Company, 1903.

Wain, John. "To Write for My Own Race." *Encounter* (July 1967): 79–85.

Webb, W. L. "Flann O'Brien's Misterpiece." (Review of *The Hard Life* by Flann O'Brien.) *Manchester Guardian* 17 November 1961.

Wilde, Oscar. *The Importance of Being Earnest*. 1899. Reprint. New York: Avon, 1965.

Index